LOST TREASURES OF SCOTLAND.

by Jack Forbes

P.B. Innis

THE DEVON PUBLISHING COMPANY, INC.

Washington, DC 20037

Copyright © 1986 The Devon Publishing Company and P.B. Innis

All rights reserved. No part of this book may be reproduced, except for the inclusion of brief quotations for review, without permission from the publisher.

Printed in the United States of America

The Devon Publishing Company Inc.
Washington, D.C. 20037

ISBN 0-9141402-03-7

INDEX

PREFACE.

THE CAMPBELL DOWRY. TICONDEROGA — PASSWORD TO DEATH.

THE GORDON TREASURE.

THE LEGEND OF THE MACDONALD GOLD.

SANDY ROBERTSON AND THE SOLID GOLD CAT.

THE CACHE OF THE CLAN MACGREGOR.

MACGREGOR'S CIPHER.

THE JEWELLED CROSS OF BLACK ISLE.

TREASURE HUNTING INFORMATION.

MAP OF SCOTLAND.

Lost Treasures of Scotland

by Jack Forbes

Every country has its share of buried and hidden treasure. Every coastline has its share of shipwrecks filled with gold. But Scotland has more than most. Its long and turbulent history of clan wars, invasions, massacres, persecutions and other tragedies, meant that people were forced to hide or bury their valuable possessions without much notice. Sometimes all who knew the secret hiding place were killed and the treasure was never recovered.

After the battle of Culloden and during the clearings of the land, many Scots fled to other countries. Some came without a penny, others brought their treasure with them and when danger engulfed them, they buried it in a secret place where it remains to this day. At least one such treasure is still waiting to be found in New York State.

Some of Scotland's lost treasures are well known and have been sought by many people. Others have been kept a secret by family and friends hoping that they will eventually find them themselves.

Since the new technics of metal detecting and air reconnaisance have made treasure hunting a more scientific venture, there has been a revival of interest in it. And, since the raising of various treasures from ships around the coasts of the British Isles and the United States, there has been new interest in sunken treasure. Modern underwater technics have made it possible to search and salvage in depths that were not possible in earlier times.

This book gives details of some lost treasures of Scotland on land and sea. Some mention of clan history and geographic details which might prove helpful are also provided.

While the author cannot guarantee that you will find a treasure, there is a guarantee that you will enjoy a vacation the the places mentioned. The scenery is splendid and, in places, weird and mysterious, especially when the mists engulf whole areas. In some of the places mentioned in this book, the traveller feels as if he has gone back to an earlier and more primitive time.

Scottish history is far more ancient than many realise. Remains of Neolithic man dated 3,500 B.C. were found in Orkney. The prehistoric Standing Stones at Callanish were built 4,000 years ago. McCullough's Tree, a 40 foot fossil, which was engulfed by lava 50 million years ago, can be seen on the Ardmeanach Peninsula when you are looking for the Macdonald gold. The Isle of Raasay contains some of the oldest plant remains ever discovered anywhere in the world. So, it is no wonder that ghostly presences seem to surround the traveller where ever he goes.

Scotland is no place for weaklings. Walking and climbing in the rugged country can tax the strongest man or woman. The tale of the Gordon Treasure in Hagberry Pot will give you an idea of what to expect!

Any trip to Scotland, especially in the out of the way places mentioned in these treasure tales, should be well planned. Public transportation is infrequent and Ferries can be booked up days ahead. Automobiles are not always available for rental when you want them so it is wise to arrange your trip in advance.

The Scottish Tourist Board has headquarters in Edinburgh at 23 Ravelston Terrace, EH4 3 EU. There are also local centers in various other places throughout Scotland which are very helpful to the traveller. Details of Bed and Breakfast accommodations all over Scotland are available from the BOOK-A-Bed facility. The Scottish Tourist Board will send booklets and pamphlets by mail on request.

While British currency is used throughout Scotland, Scottish banknotes circulate in many areas.

Once you start exploring Scotland you will want to go back again and again. Even if you don't find the treasures mentioned in this book, you will have a vacation you will never forget and come home richer than when you started out!

THE GORDON TREASURE.

The Gordon Treasure in Hagberry Pot

The Gordon treasure of gold, silver and jewels, lies in the black waters of the river Ythan, Scotland. It has lain there for hundreds of years waiting to be raised. Various members of the Clan have tried their hand at raising it, but none have succeeded so far.

The Gordons have always been known as recklessly brave, ruthless, loyal to their own and capable of villainy and excessive virtue. They can be charming and generous or cruelly calculating. More to be feared than loved, say their enemies of whom there are many.

Gordon history is filled with tragedies and victories. No Gordon ever did anything by halves. The Gordons, originally, came from the Lowlands in the 14th century and settled in Aberdeen when Sir Adam Gordon was granted lands by King Robert the Bruce, in Strathbogie.

A grandson was created Earl of Huntley. Later, a Marquessate was conferred on the 6th Earl of Huntley in 1559. The 4th Marquess had a dukedom conferred on him by King Charles the II in 1684.

The Duchess of Gordon was said to have been responsible for raising the regiment known as the Gordon Highlanders, by getting recruits to join by giving each man a kiss and a golden guinea.

It is said that the Gordons have spread all over the world adding their swashbuckling character and charm to improve the life of people everywhere.

However, of the several branches of Gordons, the one I am going to tell you about is the Gordons of Gight, of which Lord Byron, the famous poet, Gordon of Khartoum and Colonel John Gordon who was mainly responsible for the assassination of Wallenstein, were members.

The Gordons made and lost many fortunes over the years. Their raids on the property of others, brought retribution and retaliation reducing them to poverty over and over again. But, they always rose up and made a few more fortunes one way or another.

The following story of the Treasure of the Gordons of Gight, which has never been recovered from the River Ythan, is but one of the many scandals of this clan.

Although there is risk attached to searching for this treasure, the value is well worth it. When you read of my adventure on the trail of this treasure and what happened to earlier divers, you will understand why I am not going back just yet. Perhaps I am superstitious, but I can't help wondering if the Treasure is waiting for a stranger to bring it up. Since the Gordons came by it nefariously, will the Ythan only give it up to a person of good character? Or is it waiting to be raised by a another Gordon?

Anyhow, its worth trying out modern methods on this old secret.

Jack Forbes

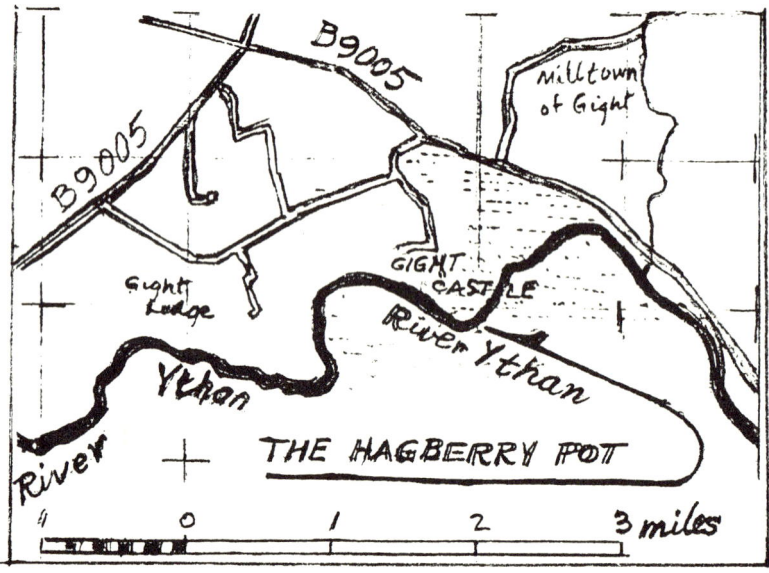

The Gordon Treasure

"How would you like to be a millionaire?"

"A millionaire? Who wouldn't?" I exclaimed, surprised at the sudden question. Although we had been talking off and on since the man joined me on the train in Edinburgh, Scotland, our conversation had had nothing to do with money. In fact we have been talking about the Gordons and the Forbes and their lands around Elgin and Gight. I had told him that I had come from the United States to look up some namesakes in the north and he mentioned he was going to stay with friends in Fyvie which was not far away.

"Well, if you're not afraid to take a bit of a risk, I can show you where to get enough treasure to make both of us millionaires."

"Treasure! Are you serious?"

"Aye," he said, "I'm deadly serious, its the treasure hid by Sir George Gordon back in 1644. I didn't intend to share it with anyone, but I need help with the project and when you told me you was a Forbes, I knew you were the one to help me. The Forbes and the Gordons inter married so much in the old days that they are pretty near the same blood."

I looked at him sharply, suspecting that he was up to something, some con game, I thought. But he appeared to be in earnest. His eyes had the feverish glitter that comes when a man gets his hands on gold or stakes his life on a chance.

"Where is this treasure and what would I have to do if I agreed to help you?" I asked, little thinking what horror and corruption lay ahead.

"Have you ever heard tell of the Hagberry Pot?"

"Hagberry Pot? No, what is it, some kind of cooking utensil?"

He laughed. It was a harsh, dry sound without humor.

"Hagberry Pot is a deep hole in the bed of the River Ythan. Its where the treasure lies waiting."

"How can you find a hole in the bed of the river? Its quite deep, isn't it? The Ythan, I mean."

"Aye, its deep, but the Pot's deeper. I can tell you don't know much about the river or you'd have heard about the Pot. You can't mistake it. The water swirls around instead of flowing right along like everywhere else. It's between Fyvie Castle and the Castle of Gight—the part they call the Black Stank. The river is deepest there and flows slow and quiet until it starts swirling into the Pot."

"Sounds a cheerful sort of place." I remarked sarcastically. "Just the spot for a suicide."

He smiled, a thin line of irregular teeth showing between his narrow lips. "It's supposed to be haunted, you know, or so people say."

"A scottish ghost? I've never seen one myself."

"It's a real one all right. Bagpipes and all."

"Where does this ghost hang out?"

"There's a great overhanging rock near the Pot called Craig's Horror. People round about named it that because a piper by the name of Craig, went into the cave there thinking he might find some clues to the treasure. But none's ever seen or heard of him since, though they say you can still hear him calling out and playing on his pipes if go round there on a dark night."

"Has anyone every gone into the cave to look for him?"

"He must have died years ago. Besides no one dares go in there any more."

"Tell me about the treasure. Whose was it? When was it lost?"

"It was back in the seventeenth century when the Castle of Gight belonged to Sir George Gordon. They say he was a big, swashbuckling character who spent his time plundering the countryside. He and his Clan got away with it for years, but one day he went too far. He took his men and on May 10th 1664, he plundered Banff and for this the Covenanters came out after him.

They fought long and hard but, in the end, Sir George had to surrender. He was taken off to Edinburgh and put in prison and the Covenanters rode on to the Castle of Gight and plundered it. But old Gordon was clever, he'd given orders that if anything went wrong and he was captured, all his treasure and valuables were to be put in chests, chained to one of the great gates of the castle and lowered into Hagberry Pot. He knew it would be safe there until he could come back and get it out.

So, while the troops smashed up everything in the Castle they never found the treasure."

"What happened to Sir George? Did he ever try to get it up?"

"He tried when he was pardoned and let out of prison, but, you know, the Pot is so deep that he couldn't find a diver willing to go down. There weren't many divers around in those days. After looking around for a year and a half, he finally found a diver willing to come to Gight to get the treasure. God knows what he promised him."

"Well, did he bring it up?"

"No, the diver went down into the Pot, but he never brought the treasure up and neither has anyone else, though plenty have tried."

"Is it really still there?"

"It must be, no one's ever brought it out."

"What was it mostly, silver, gold?"

"Silver dollars, golden goblets and plates covered with jewels. There was knives with jewelled handles, gold and silver ornaments and a casket of jewels belonging to the women of the family."

"Must be worth quite a bit today?"

"Several million, I would say, and, when you told me you had been diving for treasure in Florida, and you are a Forbes—kin to the Gordons, I considered you was the one to help me. Specially as we met by chance. If you hadn't been on this very same train in this very same carriage we never would have met. It's Fate. You're meant to do it. What do you say?" he leaned forward with that feverish glitter in his eyes again, "Fifty fifty." he urged as I hesitated.

"O.K., I'll do it." I said "I've always had a weakness for treasure, but we'd better keep it quiet. What about the rest of the Gordons, won't they be after it?"

"They might, but they're not going to get it. There's no Gordon at the Castle now and anyhow, if they haven't got it up in three hundred years, they won't get it now."

"I'll need my diving outfit and gear, that should be at Elgin already. I sent my luggage in advance. By the way, do you have any idea of the depth of Hagberry Pot?"

"I've made a lot of calculations and I know pretty well all there is to know about it. But no one really knows the depth, I'll show you my calculations and that'll give you some idea. I know exactly where the treasure is so you can go straight down to it. The Pot is not affected by the currents of the river, its too deep. Its probably lying where it sank three hundred years ago. Anyway, you can take a look at my charts and see for yourself. When can you start? Tomorrow?"

"The sooner the better. Once I'm on the track of treasure I can't think of anything else." I was getting truly excited about this thing. Even though I had some reservations about this man, there was something about him that fascinated me. Something compelling about his eyes and the way he told the Gordon treasure tale. Although I had come from the States to look up my ancestors, the treasure had pushed them out of my mind. After all, the ancestors had waited some hundreds of years, they could wait a bit longer, I thought.

"How long do you expect to stay here?"

"Only a few days, then I am going across to Ireland and then back to the States."

"In that case, it might be best to get your business done first and then we can go to Edinburgh together and share out there. People know you have a good deal of luggage so we can empty out some of your things and fill up the bags with treasure. That way it won't look suspicious."

"O.K., that's fine with me." I answered, "there's no point in letting ourselves in for a lot of trouble and taxes if we can avoid it. I'd better stay around for a couple of days and look up an ancestor or two and I'll meet you the day after tomorrow." Then I realized he hadn't given me his name.

"Did you say your name was Gordon?"

"No, my family is loosely connected with the Gordons but my last name is Smith, John Smith, a very ordinary name, I'm afraid." Again he gave me his thin smile and that strange glitter came into his eyes. I shivered and felt my skin and hackles rise.

"Someone walking over your grave?" he said noticing me shiver.

"Must be." I laughed it off, embarrassed.

"Don't worry, I don't think anyone will walk over your grave." he answered with a conviction I was to understand later.

"I'm not ready for the grave yet. I want to get that treasure first." Quickly I shook off my apprehension, "Where shall I meet you?"

He thought a moment, "You'll have to get your gear won't you? Look, here's my phone number, ring me at five tomorrow and I'll tell you where I'll pick you up."

"O.K.," I said cheerfully, peering through the window as the train slowed down, "We must be near Fyvie, aren't we?"

"Aye, we're only about a mile outside the station." He got up and pulled his bag off the luggage rack. "You won't be long now, its only about fifty miles to Elgin. You'll ring tomorrow, then?"

"Yes, at five o clock." He said a quick goodnight and vanished into the shadows of the little station.

It was quite dark when the train pulled into Elgin so I couldn't see much of the place. I was wondering how I was going to find some kind of vehicle to take me to the home of Thomas Forbes in Elgin, when a man about sixty came out of the darkness and called out,

"Ye must be Mister Jack Forbes, I'm real glad to see ye. I'm Tom Grant, friend of Thomas Forbes, I came to drive ye over. Where's your bags, mon?"

"Just these, Mr. Grant, I sent the rest on ahead. Its good of you to come and meet me—I'll carry them." I said quickly as he picked up my suitcase and camera, but he was already striding ahead. Grant led the way to an ancient auto outside the station.

"She's not much to look at, but she's a bonny engine, ye'll see." he said, stowing my things carefully in the back. I got in beside him with a feeling of well being. He seemed to be the kind of Scotsman I had read about. Upright, honest with a ruddy complexion and an air of common sense about him.

"Have you always lived here?" I asked.

"All my life and me father before me and his father before him. We don't do much moving around. We stay here or go off to America." he chuckled. "How do you like it over there? Is it all its cracked up to be?"

I answered as well as I could trying not to brag too much. He listened well, though I must admit the constant shifting of gears needed on the hilly road and the bumpy state of the surface, didn't give him much chance to talk. He asked me if I had a good journey and I told him the time passed quickly because I met a man named Smith who was related to the Gordons and who told me a lot about these parts.

"Smith," he said. "Do ye mean John Smith, a puir weak looking English mon?"

"He might be English, I don't know, but he's related to the Gordons and he spends a lot of time in Fyvie."

"Ah," said Grant noncommittally, "I know him. What's he got on his mind now?"

I hesitated. I didn't want to say anything about the treasure, but I was anxious to hear what Grant knew about Smith. There was something in the way he spoke that made me think he knew a good deal. I decided to sound him out.

"He was telling me the story of Gight Castle and Hagberry Pot."

"Aye, I'm not surprised, the puir soul has got it on his mind."

"What do you mean. Are you saying that he's crazy?"

"Well, not crazy, but he's got a grudge against the Gordons and that's all he thinks about. Did he tell you about the Pot and the treasure?"

"He told me something. Is there really treasure in there?"

"Aye, it's true enough, but there's too much death and destruction about the place for any to get hold of it. Though Smith can't rest for want of it."

"What do you mean by death and destruction?"

"Didn't Smith tell ye about the killing of the diver?"

"No, he didn't mention that he died."

"That's queer, because that's what's behind his obsession, they say. It's the one thing he mentions first of all."

"Well, he didn't tell me. What's it all about?"

"It's a sad tale, but you might as well hear it. Most people around here have forgotton it. You know the Gordons, and the Forbes, for that matter, were known for their pride and bloody deeds in those days, and when Sir George Gordon got out of prison, he made up his mind to restore the Castle of Gight better than it had been before. So he starts rebuilding and he gets this diver to come so he can bring up the treasure sunk down in the Pot.

The old man wanted the gold and silver to pay for the rebuilding and his womenfolk wanted their jewels back so they could wear them at the great party they had in mind for when the Castle was finished.

There was about two hundred people watching when the diver went down. Not one of them would have dared put a hand in the place, let alone drop down in the depths of it. They knew the Devil and his spirits used it for a meeting place. They was all watching ready to take to their heels, but drawn to the place like people watching an hanging. Well, they watched the diver out of sight and nothing happened. No devils big or little came out. Time went by and the people began to mutter that he had dropped straight into the hands of the Devil so they might as well go home. He would never come up again now that the Devil had got him. They were beginning to leave when the waters of the Pot started working and heaving as if some horrible disaster was going on underneath.

Even old Sir George feared he would never see the diver again. Then at last he appeared, but in such a terrible plight that the people all shrank back in horror. Horrible it was. That puir diver were covered with awful bruises and bleeding all over his body. He couldn't stand upright and he couldn't talk for a while, but Sir George kept at him and at last the diver gasped out that as soon as he touched the bottom of the Pot, he saw a sight which made his blood freeze.

There was a huge square rock in the river bed spread with the cloth the treasure had been wrapped in and it was set with the gold plates and the goblets and the silver from Gight. Round this table were some horrible monsters sitting on their haunches. They were like enormous toads, black as night. At the head there was a man so evil to look at that the diver knew it could only be the Devil himself. While these creatures chattered and screeched, another demon was tending the continuous blaze of sulpherous light coming out of a hole in the rock which went straight up one side of the river. This flame was heating an enormous pie dish while another demon scraped what the diver took to be big potatoes. Then he saw they were the heads of new born babies and he was scraping off the hair!! The diver was so scared he couldn't move as the cook took the pie dish to the table and the whole crew fell on it cracking the skulls with their great teeth.

The diver tried to swim away without disturbing them, but he must have made some sound because they saw him and turned on him, gabbling and screeching. They dragged him to the flames, then changed their minds and tossed him from one to another threatening to tear him to pieces, all the while yelling and laughing. Then when he was pretty near dead, they tossed him aside and told him if he ever came back they would show him more ways to die than he had ever dreamt of.

Most of the people were full of pity and wanted to get the diver into bed and take care of his wounds, but Sir George would have none of it. He did not believe such a far fetched tale and swore that the diver had made it up so that he could frighten everyone away and come back later and get the treasure for himself. He ordered the man back in the Pot and told him not to come back without the treasure.

The puir creature fell on his knees and begged Sir George to let him go in peace. He said he would not ask for pay, only to leave the place while he still had life in him. But Sir George would not hear of it. The diver pleaded and begged showing his wounds and blood.

In a terrible rage, Sir George tried to push him in but the diver clung to him so tight that Sir George would have had to go in with him, so what does he do but have the puir man taken to the Castle and tortured. One after another they pulled out his nails with pincers, but the puir diver still refused to go back into the Pot. Then they started sticking pins into the bleeding flesh where the nails had been and a few other such tricks. At last the puir man screams out that he had rather face the Devil than Sir George and they lead him back to the river bank where the people watch him fall in.

They didn't have long to wait. The Pot starts heaving and boiling and dashing against the banks. Then a blood red patch appears on the water and grows wider and wider until the whole of the Pot is red and one by one his limbs come up and then his dismembered body. They say his eyes were still open when his skull came up and he fixed them on Sir George with a look that made his face turn whiter than a corpse and he turns away without a word. He never got the treasure and, as far as I know, nobody has ever tried again."

"What a story!" I exclaimed, "but not one really believes it, do they?"

"Most people say they don't, but I've never known anyone go by there in the dark and the Gordons have been content to let the treasure lie."

"But what about Smith, he wants to get it and he's a Gordon, isn't he?"

"Smith's no Gordon nor kin to them, he's kin to the diver and he's named for him. He's got this whole tale on his mind and he's swore to vengeance, that's his trouble."

"Kin to the diver! then why—" I stopped as a terrible realization dawned on me. Of course, I was just what he had been waiting for. Not only would he get vengeance on a relative of the Gordons, but I could dive down and get the treasure and then he would do away with me and keep it all himself. There would be no questions asked, I was expected to return to the States anyway, so they wouldn't inquire about me in Scotland and my friends in the States would think I was staying longer over here. By the time they took any real steps to get in touch with me, Smith would be well away with the treasure and there would be nothing to connect him with my disappearance.

"If I was in your shoes, I'd keep out of his way." Grant went on, as if reading my thoughts.

"I certainly will." I answered fervently, my interest in the treasure was rapidly waning.

"There's the croft." Grant said as we rounded a corner and saw the lights in the distance. "Thomas is impatient to see ye."

There was a warm welcome for me inside which did much to wipe out the horror of Hagberry Pot. But I could not sleep that night for thinking of it. The more I thought, the the more certain I was that Smith intended to use me to get the treasure and do away with me. But the thought of those jewels and all that silver and gold was too tempting to turn down. After all, why should I believe Grant's tale any more than Smith's? Grant may have told me about the diver and and all that other stuff to put me off, so that I wouldn't help Smith by diving for the treasure. Maybe Grant was the one who was hoping to get it all for himself.

Monsters and demons didn't worry me. Divers in those days had no proper gear and the diver was probably badly deprived of oxygen and this would cause all kinds of halucinations. If he had heard of the demons and monsters from the natives, this would be uppermost in his mind. The wounds and lacerations could be accounted for by being dashed against the rocks by the current.

But the Pot was supposed to be so deep that there was no current down there! And what could have caused the turmoil in the water? I remembered the Loch Ness monster. Had there been some such left over prehistoric creature in the depths of the Pot? That would account for the upheaval and the wounds and, of course, the tale had most likely been embellished over the years. Common sense suggested that I make more enquiries and find out if any recent survey of the River Ythan and Hagberry Pot had been made. The whole thing might be a local myth with no truth in it whatever.

By morning, I had decided against diving for the treasure or linking up with Smith. After all, I did not have much time and it would be better to come back and do the job on my own, or with another experienced man. We could try it with grappling instruments. If this didn't work we could get hold of some modern equipment and explore the whole of the Pot.

"Did you sleep well," my host asked as I went into the cozy dining room. "You still look a bit worn out. Its a long trip up here by train."

"When I get out in this fresh air, I'll be fine. It's looks like a fine day."

"Yes, we don't get many like this, I'm afraid. We get so much mist up around here. But its never very cold. That's one thing. The

Gulf Stream comes around the north of Scotland and warms us up. I've arranged for us to go over to the rectory and see the rector. He knows a good deal about these parts. His family have been here for centuries. He said he'd be glad to go through the records with you and talk with you about your ancestors. He knows a lot more than I do."

"Thanks, I'd like to meet him. Its good of you to go to all this trouble."

"No trouble, we don't get too many visitors and it cheers me up."

Through the small panes of the window I could see a drift of heather and in the distance the ruins of the ancient Cathedral. I could hardly believe I was really here in this place that I had heard about so often from my grandfather. It was so peaceful and so quiet that Hagberry Pot and its horrors seemed like a dream. If I hadn't remembered Smith and his thin smile and glittering eyes, I would have dismissed it all from my thoughts. But for some reason, Smith's face kept coming into my mind and his voice rasping in my ears.

"It's Fate. The way we met on the train. We're meant to work on the treasure together. Why else would we be on the same train and in the same carriage?"

I had to admit it was a curious happenstance that I should meet Smith accidentally. Especially as there was no way he could have known of my interest in treasure and the fact that I had done quite a bit of digging as well as diving for sunken treasure. Most treasure hunters have a superstitious streak in their nature. Luck plays such a part in treasure hunting. Its possible to work on a code or a map for years and miss the treasure by a few feet and someone else comes along who has just heard about the thing and he'll have all the luck and hit the spot right away.

Our visit to the church put the treasure out of my mind for a bit. The rector a charming, intelligent but very talkative old man, was full of information about the Forbes from the creation up to date. He also had many anecdotes about the Forbes and the Gordon families. It seemed that they were a lively lot in Scotland in those days and the women were as bad as the men. They spent most of their time fighting one another and if they didn't have a fight going on in Scotland, many of them went overseas and fought in other lands.

"They must have been a very virile, strong and healthy race of people" I said.

"Yes, they were and most here, still are." the rector said. "I think they inherit good health or if they didn't, they died young, so only the strongest lived to breed more of the same."

"Don't you think the climate and the food has something to do with it?" Thomas Forbes asked.

"Yes, I do. The climate is bracing and the good, plain food must make a difference. All they had to march on in the old days was oatmeal and we still eat plenty of that"

"I read that doctors in the United States are telling people to eat oats to live longer. Is that so, Jack."

"Yes, they say its good for lowering cholesterol and to keep your bowels working." I answered. "But I heard its the whiskey that breeds strong men and keeps them going in good times and bad. Is it true?"

"I've never known a Scotsman yet who didn't take his daily dram or two." Thomas said with a twinkle. "I know I don't like to miss mine."

By three thirty we were back at the croft and I went up to my room to change my muddy shoes and freshen up. I kept thinking of the treasure. My curiosity and desire for wealth was too much for me to resist. Smith was probably acting in good faith and I was wrong to misjudge him. After all there was no proof of anything against him and it didn't seem reasonable to me for a man to bear a grudge over something that had happened three hundred years ago. Then I remembered that thin smile and the feverish glitter in Smith's eyes and shuddered. But I was still fascinated, I couldn't leave without doing something about it. I would never be able to rest if I didn't look into it. Ancestors could wait, my mind was on the treasure. I must have a go at it. But I'd ask Grant to go with me and keep an eye on things. Smith couldn't do much about it, if Grant turned up with me and I'd give Grant part of my share for his trouble. That would also make him keep him mouth shut.

If Smith were acting in good faith, he wouldn't object and, if he were out for my life and all the treasure, it would be good to have Grant around.

At five o'clock I dialled Smith's number and he answered immediately. Evidently he had been waiting for my call.

"I'll pick you up outside Elgin," he said. "There's a signpost about a mile on the road to Fyvie. You be there at 7 o'clock with all your baggage. Just say a friend is going to pick you up and give you a lift part way. No need to say more."

"O.K., I'll be there."

"Be sure and bring all your gear so you can go straight on after we've brought up the stuff and shared it out and don't tell anyone its me you're meeting."

"O.K. I'll see you tomorrow at 7."

Then I went to Grant and told him the story. I didn't want to worry Thomas Forbes because he was eighty years old and not too strong. I told Grant I didn't completely trust Smith and if he would come with me, I'd give him half my share of anything we brought up.

"Of course," I said "I might be misjudging Smith but when I'm under water, I'm at his mercy. I'd feel better if you just stood around and kept an eye on him. You don't have to do anything else."

Grant was silent for a while drawing on his pipe, then he said, "My advice to ye is the same as last night, Keep clear of Smith and leave the Pot to itself."

"But the treasure! I want to try for that treasure." Seeing that my mind was made up, Grant reluctantly agreed to come with me, "I'll go with ye and I'll stand by until ye're ready to go on to Ireland. Mind ye, I don't think ye'll see that treasure and ye'll never beat the Pot—but you're a true Forbes, always looking for trouble and stubborn like all of them."

Grant drove me and my gear to the signpost, then we got out and waited for Smith to appear. It was a misty, damp morning. The sky was overcast so that it was miserably dark and dreary. The whole landscape had a foreboding, chilly look. Grant was silent, sucking on his empty pipe.

We heard a car coming up the hill before we saw it. In the mist it had to be almost on top of us before we could see it was Smith.

"What the hell did you bring him for?" he muttered angrily as I stepped up to his car. "I told you not to tell anyone, you fool."

"We can trust him," I said looking Smith straight in the eye. "I need extra help with my diving gear and it'll take two men to pull that chest out of the Pot once we've located it. You couldn't do it alone."

But Smith was not to be placated. Finally, disgusted with him, I said,

"Well, O.K. if Grant doesn't come with us, I'm not going, you can get it out yourself." and I started walking back to Grant who was standing by his car.

Smith called quickly,

"Have it your own way. I was only trying to keep it quiet. Bring your stuff over, we'd better get going."

"Good morning to ye." Grant said coming over with some of my gear. Smith nodded in a surly manner as he got out and helped stow my bags and gear in the back of his car.

"So ye think ye can beat the Pot." Grant remarked as we drove along.

"We're going to try." I spoke quickly before Smith could say anything.

"A good diver shouldn't have too much trouble," Smith said, "or are you afraid of the place?"

"It's not a place I like to linger in, but I'd like to see you get the treasure out." Grant replied calmly.

"Why do they call it Hagberry Pot." I asked.

"It's because there's a whole lot of wild cherry trees around there and they say that the old Hags or witches make their evil brew out of them when they gather there for their witches Sabbaths. Pot's the name of a deep hole in a river in these parts," Grant explained.

Smith was bent over the driving wheel driving furiously along the narrow winding uneven road. I wondered where we would be if another car came to meet us. He was going far too fast, but his attitude prevented me from saying anything. The forty five miles or so to the Black Stank and Hagberry Pot were driven almost in complete silence except for the noise of the engine and the rattling of the cars body works as it bounced over the road. I was relieved to get there in one piece.

As soon as Smith stopped the car, I got out to look around. The great overhanging cliff which contained Craig's Horror loomed menacingly above casting an even deeper shadow on the sullen river. The slow, purposeful waters flowed silently hiding their secrets in the black depths.

To shake off the feeling of foreboding that seemed to stay with me, I started undressing to put on my wet suit. Smith and Grant walked over to the river bank and I could see Smith pointing out various landmarks. Then I went to the car to get my equipment, but I never got it out. A shout from Grant made me wheel around to see him fighting desperately with Smith who was trying to push him over the edge into the Pot.

"Stop! Stop!" I shouted rushing towards them, my bare feet cut by the track. Grant was almost twice Smith's age, but he was tough and Smith had his work cut out. All the same Grant was on the ground being forced backwards into the river as I got hold of Smith's collar and dragged him off Grant.

Smith's eyes were like those of a demon as he turned on me his hands at my throat. He's crazy! I realized struggling to free myself. His hands and arms were like iron, I could hardly breathe, the blood was roaring in my ears. I felt my lungs would burst. Then Grant came at him from the rear and Smith was forced to loosen his hold on my throat. I dragged in some breath but I couldn't get free. Smith was like something possessed. Grant, breathing heavily, was trying to force Smith to his knees, but we were no match for Smith in his madness. I saw Grant let go of Smith as I lost consciousness and all went black. The next thing I knew was the splash of cold water on my face. Grant was throwing it over me.

"Where is he, for God's sake."

"Rest easy, mon, I trussed him up like a chicken. He's in the back of the car. We'll drop him off at the police station when we get ye on your feet."

"How did you do it? What happened?"

"I hit him on the side of his head with a rock and knocked him out. He's out of his mind and he'd have got us both if I hadn't done it."

Slowly I got to my feet. My throat was bruised and sore and my breath came in uneven gasps. The Pot looked evil and black, the cold mist was coming up from the water. Suddenly, I wanted to get away from the horror of this place. The treasure held no more temptation for me. The Gordon's could have it.

Smith was still unconsious as we drove into Fyvie and handed him over to the authorities. I was afraid I would have to delay my return to the States as they wanted me to give evidence of Smith's attack on Grant, but they were very accommodating and let me make a sworn statement and go on my way.

Some months later, Grant wrote to me and said Smith was under psychiatric care and might be released in the care of a relative in the near future.

I have never gone back to the place. I was lucky once and don't intend to tempt Fate again. As far as I know, the treasure is still lying untouched in the bottom of Hagberry Pot.

Nobody has had the courage to dive for the treasure lately, but as the souls of women are said to be safe from the demons of the deep, perhaps a female diver might succeed where all the men have failed!!

The curse laid on the Gordons of Gight by the unfortunate diver followed through the years until the last male heir was dead. Alexander, the XI Laird drowned in the river Ythan near Hagberry Pot on Jan 24 1760. Was he searching for the treasure? The XII Laird, George Gordon was drowned in the canal in Bath, England, on Jan 9 1779. He was the last male heir and his daughter Catherine inherited the Gight estates. Catherine married the profligate John Byron and they had one son the famous poet, Lord George Byron.

John Byron quickly ran through Catherine's inheritance and the castle and land of Gight were sold to pay his debts. Thus the legendary curse was fulfilled as the herons flew from the trees of Hagberry Pot the day before the sale and neighbors recalled the verse,

When the herons leave the tree
The Laird of Gight shall landless be.

Notes re the Gordon Clan

Among the books on the various Gordons, the most useful are the three books printed for the Spalding Club of Aberdeen in 1907 entitled THE HOUSE OF GORDON.

FYVIE CASTLE by A.M.W. Stirling published by John Murray of London is most interesting and corroborates the story of Hagberry Pot.

THE COCK OF THE NORTH by the Marquess of Huntley published by Eyre and Spottiswood of London gives much of the history of the Gordons and the descent of the last King of Poland from the Gordons.

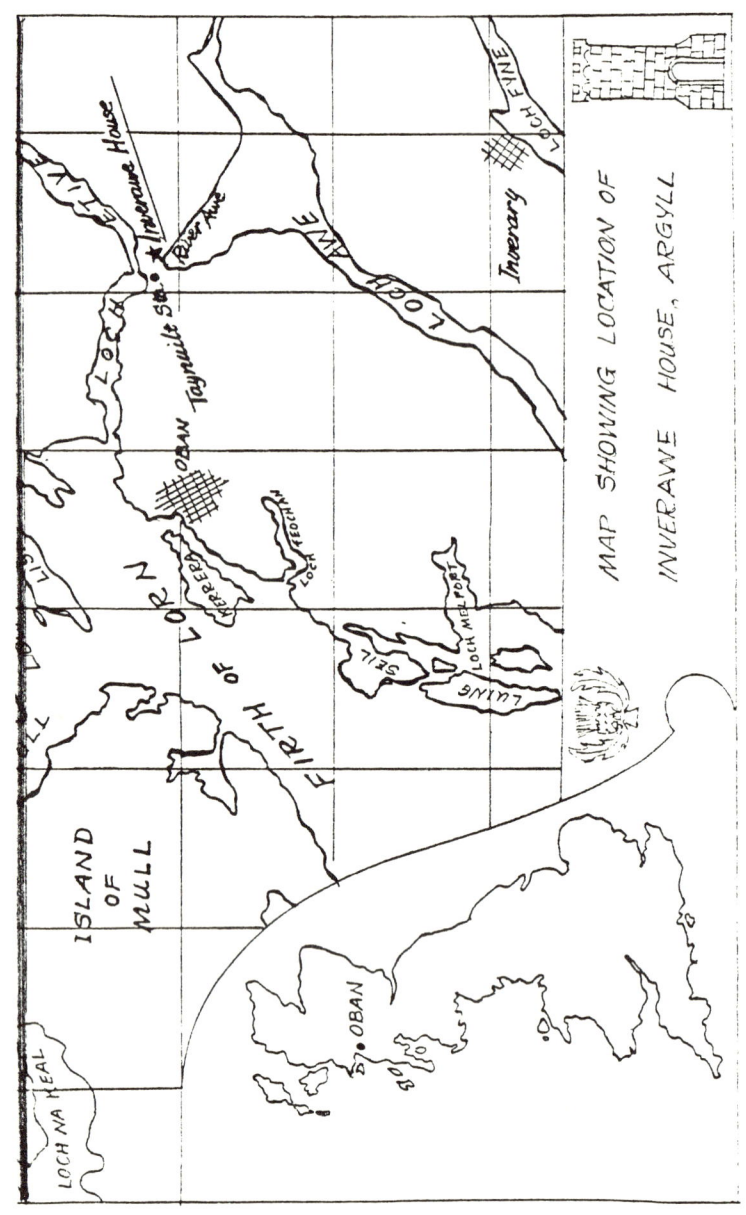

THE CAMPBELL DOWRY.

TICONDEROGA _____ PASSWORD TO DEATH.

Ticonderoga—
Password to Death

The turbulent history of Scotland sent many of its sons far from their native land. Many came to America penniless, others brought their treasure with them. Some met an untimely end and left their treasure buried in a secret place where it remains to this day.

Such a one was Duncan Campbell, Laird of Inverawe, who came to America in 1768 as colonel of the Black Watch Regiment. This Regiment had been sent to reinforce the British troops that were fighting the French and Indians. Inverawe, who knew he was accursed and was doomed to die at Ticonderoga, entrusted his Will and several bags of gold to a brother officer. The Will and the treasure were buried in a trunk somewhere near the Fort. Both Inverawe and the officer who buried the treasure, died without revealing its whereabouts.

So, somewhere not far from Ticonderoga is buried a small trunk containing a Will and several bags of gold. Since there is no record of the treasure ever being found, it would seem well worth spending a vacation searching the area with a good metal detector.

Ticonderoga—
Password to Death

The bitter wind howled around the turrets of the old castle of Inverawe blowing torrents of icy rain against the stone walls. It was a terrible night, a night for all good men to be inside by their own hearth.

Neither man nor beast could stand against this storm and even the poorest wretch was sheltering somewhere. Suddenly, a flash of lightening brought the castle into high relief against the dark sky, and with an oath, a bedraggled figure flung himself against the iron studded door and began desperately banging on it with his bare hands. Even though he could hardly stand upright, he kept looking fearfully over his shoulder as he continued his desperate assault on the door.

Inside the castle, Duncan Campbell, Laird of Inverawe, leapt to his feet as the knocking echoed through the hall. For a moment he stood irresolute beneath the tattered battle honors and the arms of his ancestors. Except for two ancient retainers who had long since retired to a far part of the castle, he was alone. Inverawe was a courageous man but the knocking sent a chill to the very marrow of his bones. When it continued more insistent than ever, Campbell snatched up a lantern and started to the door.

Only a desperate man or a band of outlaws would be demanding entrance at this hour on such a wild night. And there were plenty of these around in this year of 1748. The battle of Culloden had ruined Scotland. Hunted men lurked in the hills, and families starved in the crofts. No man knew when his turn would come so few refused shelter when it was asked. A man might be on the run himself the next day, so most would share their last morsels of food and drink if called on.

Campbell knew well the danger of opening the door. It might be himself they were after. Then again, it might be a friend or kinsman needing help. Without any more hesitation he raised the bar and, opening the door, he saw the bloodstained clothing and torn kilt of a stranger standing there.

"Let me in, for God's sake," the man begged harshly. "They're right on my heels."

Without a word, Campbell opened the door wider and the man staggered in.

"I canna go farther." he gasped, "will ye shelter me?"

"Who's after ye." Campbell asked.

"There's two men—armed. There were three of them, but I killed one when they started arguing with me. I was alone and they were three, so I had to look out for myself. Will ye shelter me?" he demanded, looking around the stout walls of the old hall.

"Aye, I'll shelter ye." Campbell replied, the hospitality for which he was known sounding in his voice. While some of the Clan Campbell were a harsh and cruel lot, the Laird of Inverawe was known as a just and good man whose word was to be trusted.

"Swear on your dirk then!" the stranger urged. "Your dirk, man!"

Campbell was surprised and insulted. His word was never doubted. His honor was almost a legend. But seeing the terror in the man's face, and realizing that he did not know he was the Laird of Inverawe, Campbell put his hand on his dirk and swore to shelter the stranger who had come to his gate. The man breathed more easily. He knew that Campbell would never betray him now that he had sworn the most solemn oath a Scotsman could make.

"Come with me," Campbell said, "I'll take you where you will be safe forever if need be."

Quickly, the stranger followed as Campbell led him along winding corridors, down narrow steps until they finally came to a secret cell in the depths of the castle.

"I'll be soon back with food for ye." Campbell said as he closed the entrance.

No sooner had Campbell reached the hall again when an even louder knocking came on the gate and Campbell knew the pursuers had arrived. As he went to open up the door, the same chill of foreboding came over him and he wondered if he would live to see the end of this dreadful night. As he lifted the lantern and opened the door, the water falling on the stones seemed to turn to blood as the light caught it.

"Are ye the Laird of Inverawe?" the two armed men demanded.
"I am."

"We have bad news for ye. Your cousin Donald is murdered and we are looking for his murderer."

Campbell looked at them with horror. His cousin dead!

"Where? What happened?"

"We were riding back with him from Aberdeen and were set upon by thieves. Donald was shot and killed but we had our pistols ready and shot the horses from under two of them and wounded another. The rest galloped off. We tried to catch those on foot but we lost them in the darkness, though we think one came this way. Have ye seen any stranger?"

Campbell stood in silent horror as the terrible realization crept over him. His cousin Donald was dead and he had sworn on his dirk to shelter his murderer!! Sick at heart, but held by his oath, Campbell said stiffly,

"I have seen no one."

"Then we'll be on our way. Ye'll be wanting to avenge your kinsman, so we'll not hold ye." And they turned and went back into the stormy night. The sound of their horses muffled by the wind and rain.

When they were gone, Campbell, Laird of Inverawe, put the bar across the door and strode back into the hall. A hideous black rage against the stranger seized his mind and an even more terrible grief for the cousin he could never avenge. Frantically, Campbell's brain strove to find away out of the web he was tangled in. But there was no way out. The two irreconcilable facts stamped themselves deeper and deeper on his mind.

His cousin must be avenged but his oath must not be broken.

What in God's name could he do? He considered killing the man or leaving him to starve. No one would ever know. But he knew that his conscience would not let him rest if he harmed the murdering wretch. An oath to shelter meant sheltering from all harm.

Frustrated and embittered, Campbell stirred the dying fire. He was shivering with cold. The candles were dying, only the lantern gave a flickering light. He picked up the goblet from the table and finished the wine he had been drinking when the murderer knocked on the door. Then he remembered he had promised the man food, but, by the Rood, he thought, I'll go to Hell sooner than look on his face again tonight. He must wait 'til the morning. By then my mind will be better able to deal with it all. Campbell refilled the goblet and gulped down the wine. It was the last bottle of a gift from one of his friends in France and he had been trying to make it last, but now he felt the need of it. Maybe it would help him sleep or sharpen his wits enough to find a way out of the dilemna.

At last he managed to drag himself to bed, but he could not sleep. He tossed and turned for hours then, just before dawn, he fell into an uneasy sleep. Afterwards, he was never sure whether he woke up or whether something awakened him, but he knew it was not a dream. Something or someone touched his shoulder with a stealthy hand. Immediately, Campbell shot upright in the bed, an awful terror gripping him as he saw a tall figure standing over him. It was the murdered Donald standing at his bedside! Not flesh and blood, but a ghostly shade spoke to him in a hollow, accusing voice.

"Inverawe, Inverawe, blood has been shed. The murderer must not be shielded. Ye must avenge me. I am your kinsman. The debt must be paid."

Shuddering, Campbell fell back and pulled the cover over him in a vain effort to hide the thing from sight. But the voice was not to be denied it went on and on, finally dying away into the distance. Campbell was desperate. Either way he betrayed a trust. As Laird of Inverawe, his cousin had the right to demand vengeange of him and he had no right to deny it. As Laird of Inverawe, who had given his oath to shelter a stranger, he could not kill the murderer or betray him.

Hour after hour, his brain turned over the bitter choice. At last, Campbell decided that surely the tie of blood was the thicker and, though he could not kill the murderer, yet he would refuse to shelter him any longer. So Campbell went to the secret place, determined to send the man on his way. As he opened the door, the man stepped forward and snatched the food from him, murmuring his thanks as he swallowed it. Campbell stood waiting for him to satisfy his hunger, then he said,

"I can shelter you no longer." The man looked up, pale with terror.

"You swore on your dirk. You can't refuse me. Does your oath mean nothing to ye?"

"It was my cousin you murdered. Though my oath keeps me from vengeance, I will not harbor you."

"Your cousin!" the stranger exclaimed. "I was ignorant of it" Then he went on harshly, "Your oath binds you, kinsman or not."

"I will not shelter you," Campbell said again. His knuckles were white as he clenched his hands to prevent himself from striking the man. "I will not betray you, but I will not shelter you. You must go."

"If you send me from this place, where can I go? You well know there is no other shelter. You may as well kill me here and be done with it." Bitterly Campbell admitted this was true. Inverawe Castle stood on the lonely banks of the River Awe, almost surrounded by hills and moorlands. If he turned the man out, he would die at the hands of his pursuers or from starvation and the bitter weather. Then he remembered a cave in the mountains the Campbells used for fugitives years before.

"I'll take you where you will be safe," he said. "But I cannot keep you under my roof."

Seeing that Campbell's mind was made up, the stranger agreed to go with him to the mountain. Campbell gave him provisions and a tartan, and left him to himself.

That night Campbell was again awakened by the chill of the ghostly hand on his shoulder. The same appalling sight met his faltering eyes. Donald stood there sterner and more accusing than before, his wounds oozing blood. He repeated the words of his previous visit.

"Inverawe, Inverawe! blood has been shed. Ye must avenge me. The murderer must not be shielded. Avenge me, your kinsman!"

Then Campbell knew he must break his oath to the stranger, or he would never know peaceful rest again. As soon as it was light he hurried to the cave. But it was empty. There were no signs of the stranger and no message to tell what had become of him.

Back at the castle, Campbell could neither work nor rest. That night when he tried to sleep, something kept him from closing his eyes. He waited for the touch of that ghostly hand until it was almost a relief when Donald appeared again. This time he was less stern, but of a horrible paleness.

"Farewell, Inverawe," he said, "We will not meet again until you set foot on Ticonderoga. There you will pay the price." And he was gone as he had appeared, without sound or movement.

As the years went by, Campbell gradually pushed these events out of his mind. Campbell never heard from the stranger or his cousin Donald again. He prospered and the castle was refurbished. He married an agreeable lady of wealth and they had several children, but the strange word Ticonderoga, which he had never heard before, was fixed in his memory. He knew with an awful certainty that this place was his doom. None of his friends or his family knew of this place, and they tried to make him forget it.

"It is something your brain made up when you were distraught." some said.

Campbell had told his wife the tale before they were married, as he felt she should be made aware of the curse that had been laid upon him. After all, she had the right to know that death and ruin could come any day. But his wife did not treat is seriously.

"It was a dream, you were so upset by the death of your cousin and having to shelter his murderer that it was on your mind and came out in the dream. There's no place in the world with a name like that, and if there is, we won't let you go there."

But nothing anyone said removed the awesome sound of that name, Ticonderoga. Was it something his distraught brain had made up or was it real? Although Inverawe wanted to believe the whole thing was a dream, he knew it was real and that some place, somewhere was Ticonderoga waiting for him. It made no difference that he was jokingly told by friends,

"You're lucky, when you know the place you are going to die, all you have to do is stay away from it and you'll live forever."

Years went by and Campbell, who had joined the Black Watch, as the Forty Second Regiment was called, was kept busy keeping order in the turbulent Highlands of Scotland. He was a brave officer and a good leader, his men would follow him anywhere and, in time, he became a Major in the regiment.

It was about two years after the French and British Wars broke out in America, that the Black Watch was ordered to join other British troops going over to reinforce the provincial forces. Campbell was glad of the opportunity of going to America and of fighting the French. His son, Alexander Campbell went with him.

But the Lady of Inverawe did not want her husband or her son to go,

"Do not go so far away, we need you here, don't go to that America, I beg of you. Stay here with me." his wife urged.

"But, my dear, you know its my duty to go. There's nothing I can do about it unless I resign from the regiment and, to do that when ordered to fight, would bring our name into dishonour, you must know that."

His wife was silent. She had an awful presentiment that if he went to America, he would never return. Although she had spoken lightly of the curse laid upon her husband by Donald, she lived in dread of it. Was there such a place as Ticonderoga in America. What if Inverawe or Alexander were captured by Indians or the French, who would rescue them or pay their ransome?

At last, after her repeated pleadings, Inverawe agreed to take some bags of gold in case he should be held for ransome—though, as he told his wife, this was part of her dowry and was meant for her to live on if anything should happen to him.

"I don't care what happens to me if you are gone, so please take care. Take great care of yourselves and then you can bring my dowry back to me intact." And she embraced her husband and son with many tears and blessings.

The Black Watch fought with the greatest bravery and success in America and Inverawe and his son kept safe and well. Then, in 1758, Campbell heard to his unutterable horror that his regiment was ordered to the attack on Ticonderoga!! All the events of the past came back to his mind with a horrifying clarity. He felt powerless. His face was haggard as he told his brother officers where they were ordered. Those few who knew his story tried to cheer him. But it was useless. He was calmly obsessed with his doom. Nothing could shake his conviction that he would die on the field. But why in this place? Why had his cousin decided on this place?

Inverawe had no fear for the outcome of the battle. The British had 15,000 troops and Lord Howe, the most brilliant leader and the most popular general of the time, to lead them. Although Lord Abercromby was commander-in-chief, he left it all to Howe. With Howe leading and with the splendid body of troops, 6337 of whom were regulars, the French would have no chance. Why should he be so despondent? There was every chance he would come through this battle unscathed and then the spell would be broken and he need never fear the word Ticonderoga again.

But, just to be sure, he gave his Will and the bags of gold to a brother officer who had been wounded and so would not be in the battle, with instructions to use it for ransome if either he or his son were captured. Or, if he Inverawe, were killed, the Will and the gold should be handed to his son. If for any reason the officer could not carry out these plans, he was to bury the gold and the Will in a small trunk, in a place known to them both.

Inverawe did not want his son to know how obsessed he was with the curse, he was afraid it might make his son so concerned about his father that he would be careless about his own safety.

As they moved up to Lake George, Campbell was cheerful, urging on his men and even joking about the spoils of victory. All was pointing to a great victory and the men were spoiling for battle.

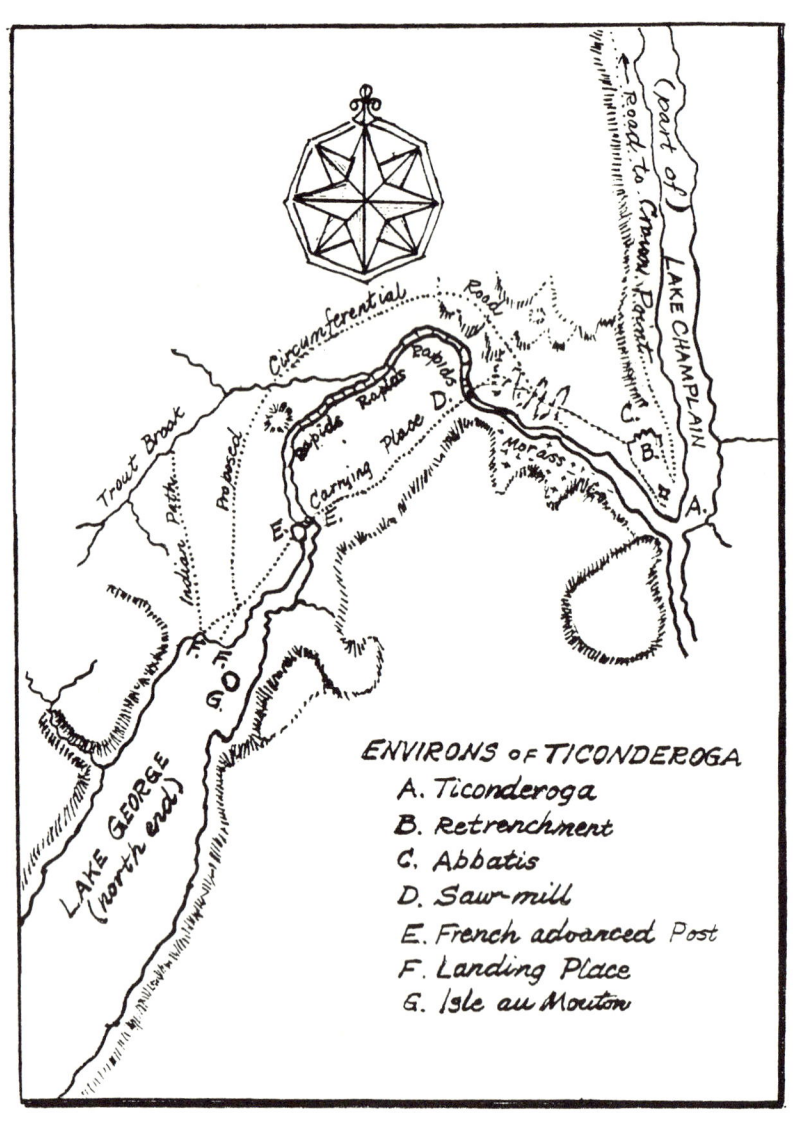

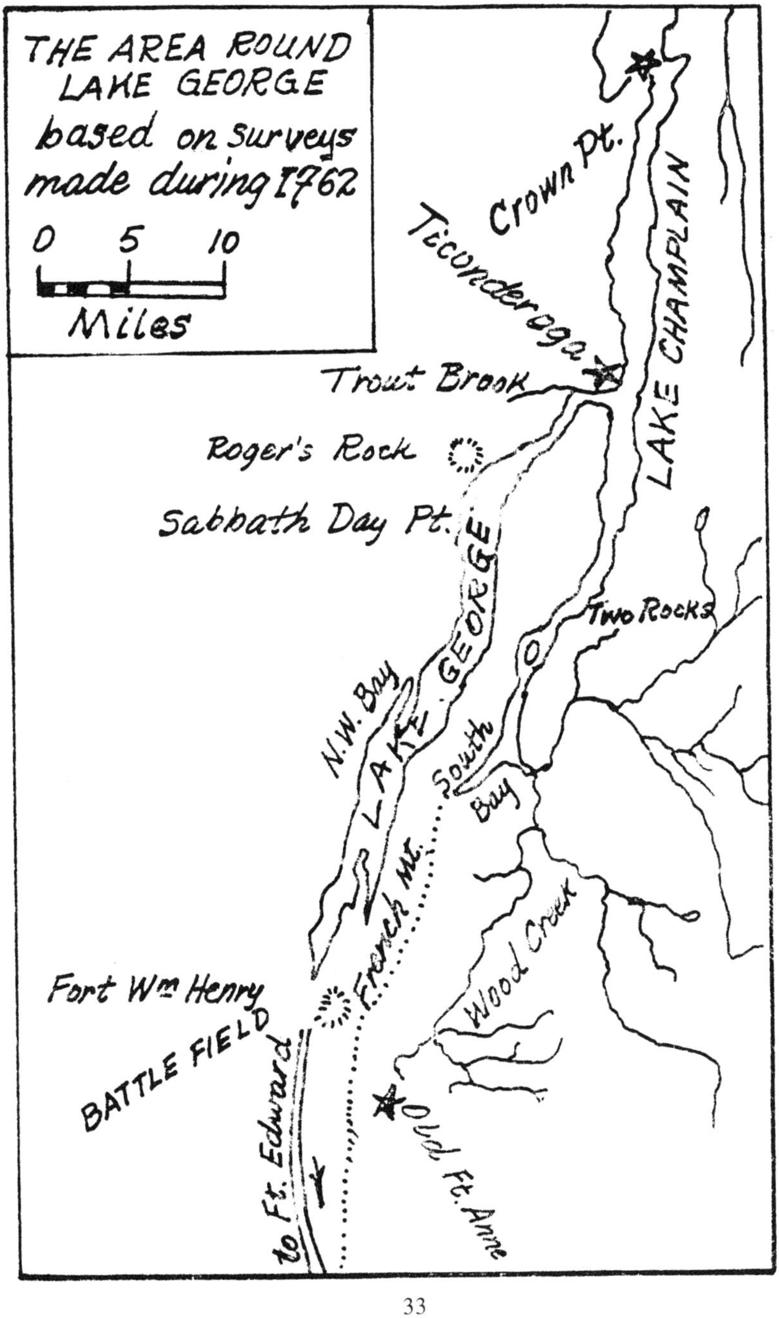
THE AREA ROUND LAKE GEORGE
based on surveys made during 1762
0 5 10
Miles
Crown Pt.
Ticonderoga
LAKE CHAMPLAIN
Trout Brook
Roger's Rock
Sabbath Day Pt.
LAKE GEORGE
Two Rocks
N.W. Bay
South Bay
French Mt.
Wood Creek
Fort Wm Henry
BATTLE FIELD
to Ft. Edward
Old Ft. Anne

It was July 4th 1758, when Abercromby embarked his troops on Lake George, on board 900 bateaux and 135 whale boats, with provisions, artillery and ammunition. Several cannon were mounted on rafts to cover the landing to be made the next day. This landing took place without any opposition, the enemy abandoning their advance post without firing a shot.

Campbell and his men were elated. This was to be an easy victory.

Then the dread news came. Lord Howe, who was leading a small advance party, was dead. Killed in a confused skirmish with the French in thick woods. This made a deep impression on the men. Campbell's mood changed to a deep gloom, and his worst fears came back. One officer, who knew his story, tried to convince Campbell that Ticonderoga was really Fort George not Ticonderoga at all, but although Inverawe smiled, he knew it would make no difference.

The night before the final assault began, Campbell was sleeping in his tent when a touch awakened him. This time he did not jump up. He was not even alarmed. Calmly he looked on the shade of his cousin Donald. Calmly he heard him say,

"Inverawe! Inverawe! We meet at Ticonderoga" then, before Campbell could speak, Donald was gone.

Fort Ticonderoga stood on a tongue of land between Lake Champlain and Lake George. It was surrounded on both sides by water and on the other side was a marsh. The French, under General Montcalm, had built a great breastwork of felled pine trees. Huge felled trees and sharpened branches covered the hill up to the breastwork. Montcalm's rear was unprotected, but he counted on Abercromby making his usual frontal attack. Abercromby fell into the trap. Although the battle began with the advantage of numbers and equipment on the British side, without Lord Howe the troops lacked leadership. Abercromby had never inspired men and, without Howe's guidance, he was lost. Abercromby ordered the British to charge the breastwork with bayonets. With wasted, reckless valor the troops stormed the hill, caught in a deadly crossfire as they tripped over the felled trees and were entangled in briars and sharpened branches. Campbell and his Highlanders fought with a stubborn bravery, the dying urging on their comrades, telling them not to waste time on them but to remember the honor of their country and take the hill.

Inverawe fought like a man possessed. He was determined that he would die face to face with the enemy. The Highlanders, with twenty-five of their officers killed or wounded, actually reached the breastwork when Inverawe was hit by a shot which almost tore off his arm. Somehow his clansmen got him off the field in spite of his urging them to save themselves.

"Leave me. Take care of yourselves."

"You're alive and we will get you away from this place so you have nothing to fear. You will recover away from here."

They carried him off the battle field convinced that if they could get him away from Ticonderoga alive, the curse would be thwarted and he would be safe. At Fort Edward a surgeon attended to his wounds and there was hope for his full recovery.

But it was not to be. Campbell of Inverawe lingered for nine days suffering horribly. Then seeing that the arm was gangrenous, it was decided to amputate it to save his life. Weakened by loss of blood, Inverawe died a few hours after the operation.

He was buried near Fort Edward. His gravestone reads

'Here lies the body of Duncan Campbell of Inverawe, Esquire, Major to the old Highland Regiment, aged 55 years, who died the 17th of July, 1758 of wounds received in the attack of the Retrenchment of Ticonderoga, on the 8th July 1758'

Alexander Campbell was also wounded, but he recovered enough to travel back to Scotland. The officer with whom Inverawe had left the Will and the gold was ordered back to Britain and, in the confusion after the battle, he had trouble contacting Alexander, so he buried the Will and the gold in the place agreed upon with Inverawe. Then he sent a letter to Alexander by a soldier stating that his father's Will and valuable property had been buried in the place agreed upon.

But Alexander, of course, did not know the place. His father had never told him. With much difficulty he traced the officer only to find that he had died of his wounds en route to England. The Lady of Inverawe sent a kinsman back to America to try to find the place, but without success.

As far as we know, the Will and the gold are still buried in the little trunk awaiting a finder.

Notes re Duncan Campbell of Ticonderoga

Among the sources used for this story are the Campbell archives,

Letter from Lord Abercromby to Pitt 19 Aug 1758.

Letter from James Campbell to Dean Stanley 1878,

the Regimental history and

The London Magazine 1758.

Ransom money

Some people have questioned whether ransome money was carried by officers, but there are precedents in historic and present times. Some of the Crusaders are known to have carried gold and precious stones and, in World War II, U.S. Navy fliers were supplied with two ounces of gold and a little knife to shave off pieces to buy their way out, or to get assistance if they were wounded, should they be shot down in China.

THE LEGEND OF THE MACDONALD GOLD.

Skye & Surroundings

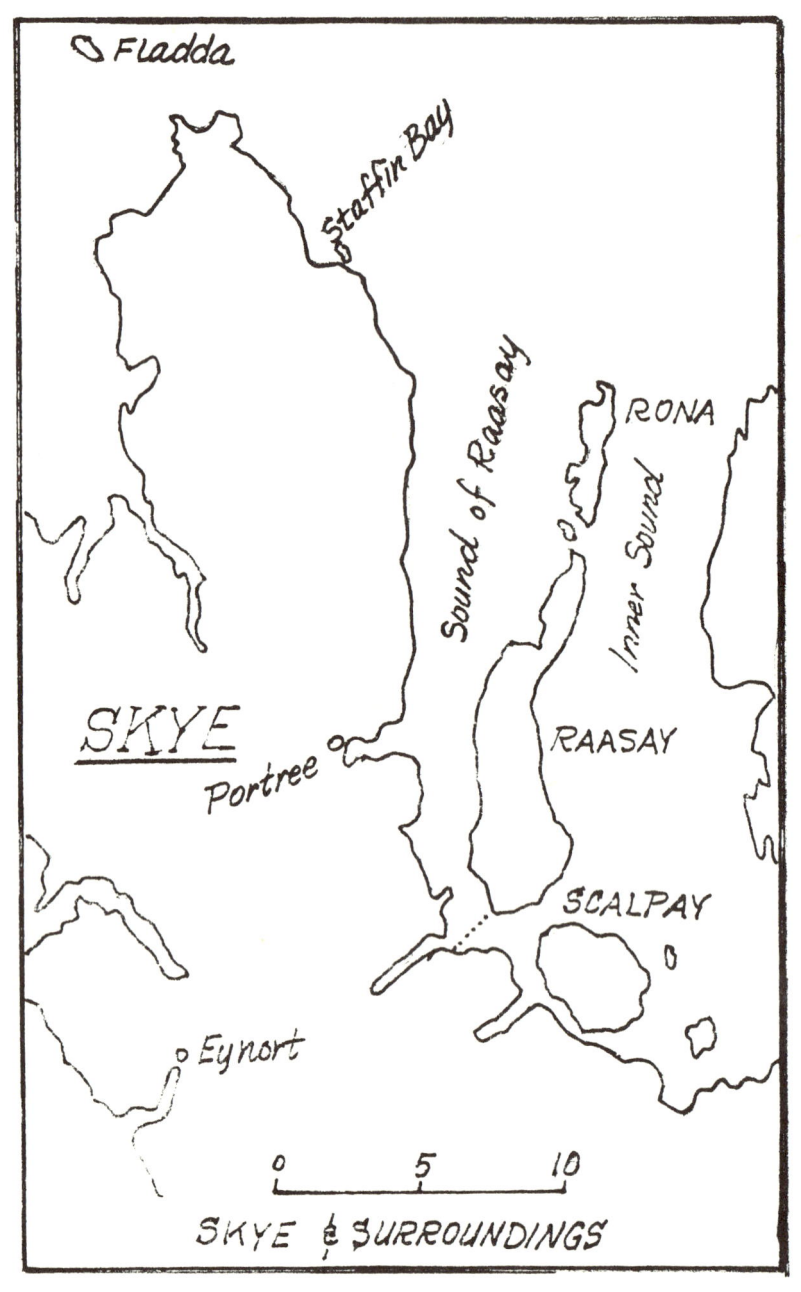

The Legend of the MacDonald Gold

In the early days, the Clan Donald was the most powerful and influential in all Scotland. They were Kings of the Isles and of Man, Lords of the Isles and Earls of Ross.

The clan was founded by Somerled, a leader of obscure origin who drove out the Norwegian pirates and relieved the people of the Isles and parts of the Scottish mainland, from constant terrorism and attack.

Close links were kept with Norway, however, and Somerled arranged to marry the daughter of the Norwegian who, at that time, was King of the Isles. Through this marriage, the titles came to the MacDonalds.

The Clan flourished and several branches developed, the three most prominent being the MacDonalds of Ardnamurchan, the MacDonalds of Clanranald and the MacDonalds of Sleat. But through warfare and treachery of one kind and another, the power of the MacDonalds was broken and much of their lands lost.

In 1692 the Chief of the Glencoe MacDonalds and nearly all his clan were massacred by the Campbells of Glenlyon.

Shortly after this, Ian one of the few survivors, resolved to ally himself with the Norwegians once more. He thought that with Norwegian support he could get back the MacDonald lands and wreak his revenge on the Campbells. Ian knew that Eyoff one of the principal chieftains of Norway, had a daughter of marriageable age and, he thought, what could be better than to arrange a marriage between his son Donald and this girl who was said to be very beautiful.

Donald MacDonald was a handsome, upright young man of 26 years. He had a commanding air tempered by a winning personality. They would make a splendid pair. The chief's daughter would surely fall in love with such a man. It was, of course, not suitable for Donald to go in person to ask for the Norwegian maiden's hand, so Ian MacDonald decided to send his young nephew, Grant to Norway to carry the offer of marriage and a portrait of Donald, to chief Eyoff.

After consulting with members of the Clan, a letter was drawn up stating the benefits to both sides. The Norwegians would regain their foothold in the Isles and the MacDonalds restore their own lost power and lands. The young couple would assuredly have many children and lay the foundations of a great dynasty.

Presents of gold and precious stones were prepared so that chief Eyoff and Ymirl, his daughter would see that she would be well provided for.

Grant was not too pleased with the task he was given by his uncle, but he dutifully prepared himself to do his best, knowing well that the MacDonalds must have a strong ally if they were to regain their power ever again.

So, he set sail with five companions and a good crew. Although the North Sea is always stormy and rough, even in summer, Grant's ship was sturdy and they arrived on the coast of Norway without serious incident.

It took several days of travel to reach the castle of Eyoff where Grant and his companions were received in a friendly fashion, but with some suspicion. This suspicion was put to rest when Chief Eyoff read the message Ian MacDonald had sent and saw the rich presents Grant had brought.

"I have news that the MacDonalds are destroyed, that they will never again regain their power. How say you to that, young sir?"

"It is true that we have suffered great misfortune, but we are far from being ruined. We have a strong following and with your help we are sure we can regain our power and once more become Lords of the Isles."

"My daughter may not wish to leave her home to marry a stranger."

"Scots and Norwegians can never be strangers to one another and our families have intermarried together in the past."

"Tonight you will meet my daughter and you can speak to her of your land. Do not mention the marriage, I will do that myself when the time comes, but tell her how life is there. Tell her about yourself and your family. I must consult others regarding the marriage and all it would mean, so I do not want it mentioned yet."

Grant replied that all would be done as his host wished and he was looking forward to meeting the fair maiden Ymirl.

That evening Grant dressed in all his regalia. He knew he looked extremely well in his Scottish full dress. Even though he was not as tall or as handsome as his cousin Donald, he cut a fine figure in his tartan.

Entering the great hall where the feast for the visitors was prepared, Grant felt he could hold his own with anyone. When he was with his cousin or his uncle, he always felt inferior. They were taller, more commanding, more easy in their manner than Grant. He could not talk with everyone as they did, but tonight he felt a newfound dignity. That is until he set eyes on the Fair maiden Ymirl.

He had never even dreamt of anyone so beautiful. Slender and graceful as a flower in springtime, Ymirl was all white and gold. Her skin was like the snow on the mountains and her hair of a rich pale gold, her eyes as blue as a Highland Loch in summertime. Her gown was white with golden embraidery and around her throat was a necklet of gold and gems.

"This is my wife, the Lady Mara and my daughter Ymirl." Eyoff said.

"She is so beautiful!" Grant stammered, "so very beautiful."

"You mean the Lady Mara, of course." Eyoff smiled.

"Yes, no, yes—my lady I am most honored to meet you." Grant struggled to pull himself together and act properly. He had never been overcome by female beauty before and realized that his new found dignity was deserting him.

"We are glad to see our friends from Scotland and to hear about your family." The Lady Mara said.

Somehow Grant managed to pay his respects to the various members of Eyoffs family and others who had been invited, then to his utter delight, he was seated next to Ymirl. She turned to him and smiled, her eyes meeting his and Grant felt his heart go out to her, he hardly heard her question,

"Is this your first visit to our land?"

"Yes, my family has told me about it, but this is the first time I have been here."

"Your voyage was good."

"Very good."

He found it so easy and pleasing to talk with her and by the time he was shown to his sleeping room, he was hopelessly and completely in love with her. O, God, he thought, she is to be my cousin's wife she can never be mine. I can never marry her. What has happened to me? I must control my feelings. Its her beauty that overcame me. Besides I am already betrothed to Mistress Mary Forbes. What has come over me? I'm bewitched, that's what it must be.

During the next few days Eyoff was conferring with his followers and friends and so Grant and the fair Ymirl were thrown together most of the time. They were never completely alone, but Ymirl's waiting women always kept at a discreet distance.

Ymirl showed Grant her favorite parts of the gardens, she took him riding in the surrounding countryside and even arranged a short expedition into the mountains. Although Grant knew he was falling more and more deeply in love with her, he was so fascinated by Ymirl that he was completely helpless to break away.

One evening as Ymirl was being dressed by her women for the evening meal, she saw two of the maidens whispering and smiling as they looked at her.

"What are you talking about? What makes you smile?"

The maidens fell silent immediately and looked guilty, which made Ymirl more curious than ever.

"Come, you must tell me."

"It was nothing, mistress, just something we overheard."

"About what?"

"It was about the scottish Lord, mistress."

"What do you know of him, tell me quickly." The maidens looked at each other and then one said,

"Let's tell her."

"No, no."

"Tell me quickly, or I'll have you both whipped." Ymirl said, out of patience with them.

"It's only gossip, something we heard the Chief's men talk about. They said, the chief, your father, is consulting about your marriage."

"My marriage!" Ymirl exclaimed, "my marriage, you mean with the scottish Lord?"

"Yes, mistress, Did you not know?"

Ymirl was silent. Her parents had said nothing about marriage. They had only told her that the MacDonalds wanted to make an alliance with them again. Ymirl knew that such an important thing as a marriage would have to be agreed upon by all her father's supporters. If they were against it, no more would be said. Her parents would wait until the discussions were over before telling her anything about it. It was the custom for marriages to be arranged by parents when lands and riches were part of the dowry.

All that evening Ymirl thought of nothing but the marriage. What would it be like to be married with the scottish Lord? She would have to live in Grant's land, to bear his children, to leave her parents and friends. She kept looking at Grant under her eyelashes and shivered deliciously. She was already half in love with him and she felt she could happily go with him anywhere. But, of course, she said nothing and, although she tried to be as natural as possible, Grant felt there was a change in her.

After the evening meal was over, as Ymirl said goodnight to Grant, he took her hand and kissed it fervently. Their eyes met for a moment, she gently pressed his hand in return and then she was gone.

That night in their separate beds, each lay thinking of the other and imagining the delights of being together.

Next day Ymirl was hurrying to meet Grant when her father sent for her. She was not prepared to find her parents surrounded by friends and relatives talking with Grant and his entourage.

"Come, my daughter, we have something important to tell you."

Ymirl's heart leapt. Her marriage to Grant must have been arranged! With a smile she listened as her father read the messages from Ian MacDonald. There was much about the two countries and then the terms of the marriage contract were read to her. Suddenly, shock and horror flooded Ymirl—our son Donald MacDonald with your daughter, the fair maiden, Ymirl—Donald MacDonald! There must be a mistake. It was Grant she was to marry. Her eyes flew to Grant but he was not looking at her.

"Father," she cried, "who is this Donald?" Her father stopped reading,

"Donald MacDonald is the son of Sir Ian MacDonald, a cousin of Grant here who came to carry the messages from his uncle, Sir Ian. We have decided that the marriage would be greatly to the advantage of both our families. Donald is handsome, a fine young man." The chief turned to a servant nearby, "Bring the portrait to the Lady Ymirl."

The man brought the portrait and held it up in front of Ymirl and mechanically her eyes swept over it. But all she could see was Grant's face. Pulling herself together, she looked again and saw the handsome face of Donald looking back at her. It was this Donald she had to marry not Grant. He was only the messenger. How could she have made such a mistake! She had practically thrown herself at Grant thinking he was the one she was to marry. What must he think of her? Ashamed and bewildered, she said quietly,

"He is very handsome as you say, father."

"Yes, and he has sent you many presents of gold and jewels, my dear. We must prepare presents for you to send to him. Now we must prepare letters and your mother wants to speak with you about many things."

"Come, my dear." Her mother said putting her arm around Ymirl. "Let us go to my room."

When they were in her mother's sitting room, Ymirl let her feelings go,

"How can I marry with a stranger, mother? How can I love someone I have never seen?"

"You will grow to love him, my dear. Such a marriage is good for both our families. You will be happy, I am sure of it. It is usual for a maiden in your position to marry with someone chosen by the parents. Often they do not meet until the wedding, but usually they are very happy together. I did not meet your father until a week before the wedding. I felt just as you do, but as you see, we are happy together. In any case, the wedding will not take place for a year. You will have time to accustom yourself to it."

Ymirl knew there was nothing to be done and she was so ashamed of her forward behavior with Grant, that she avoided him and only saw him at the evening meal until he was leaving. Then she only bade him a cold farewell and a safe journey.

Grant sensed her coldness but, even in the depths of his despair, he realized this was the best way to part. They could have no future together. He must get Ymirl out of his mind and so he left without a backward look.

It was autumn when Grant reached home again. Everyone was delighted with the success of his mission and he was greeted with congratulations from all.

"Your were a good emissary, Grant. You brought the right answer in a very short time. You have started the MacDonalds back to their former glory," his uncle said. "Now we must make haste with the wedding preparations. A year will pass too quickly."

But for Grant the year went too slowly. Every hour away from Ymirl was agony. He alternated between passionate desire and resentful feelings of being bewitched. Why else would he be so besotted over a woman?"

By the time the year had passed, Grant's feelings had grown quite beyond control. It was as if Ymirl controlled his whole existence. She was never out of his thoughts. He had to possess her no matter what the cost and he formulated a secret plan which, although it would bring sorrow and the loss of all the MacDonald hopes, he intended to carry it out.

Enthusiastically he went about the preparations to fetch Ymirl for the wedding. His uncle couldn't help noticing all the time he put in supervising the ship's outfitting and particularly the quarters Ymirl would occupy.

"The MacDonald's will be forever grateful to you, Grant, you have done far beyond what I expected to make a success of our plans and hopes. When you return we must see that you and Mistress Forbes celebrate your wedding with all extravances we can prepare."

"You are most gracious and generous, I hope that the plans go well and the seas are free of storms."

"It is a good time of the year, but the sea is to be watched every minute. The storms come up so quickly and often without warning."

"The captain is experienced, I am told."

"He is the best we have. He will take no 'risks.'"

It seemed to Grant that the Fates were on his side. The voyage was good, a following wind helped them arrive in the Norwegian port in record time. Although Grant could scarcely wait to see Ymirl, he forced himself not to show his obsessive need for her. In order to carry out his plan, no one must suspect that his feelings for Ymirl were more than those of a cousin. But, when he saw her again, he feared his passion would consume them both.

"Are you ill, my friend." Eyoff asked, noticing Grant's pallor and burning eyes. "It seems the journey has been too exhausting for you. You must rest."

"It will pass. It's a fever I have had for some weeks. I am used to it. But I will take your advice and rest for a while." And, without speaking to Ymirl, he followed a servant to the room prepared for him.

After taking some wine and resting alone, Grant was able to control his feelings and he vowed he would not let Ymirl's presence affect him again. He would be patient. His plans were made and he would possess her in time. All he had to do was carry out the carefully laid plans. He knew he could not fail.

By the time he reached the Hall for the evening meal he was in full control and was able to greet Ymirl with suitable decorum. Ymirl kept her eyes down and responded quietly and graciously to his greeting. She accepted the messages from the MacDonalds with prepared words of thanks and Grant could not tell whether the feelings he knew she had for him last year, were still there or not. But it didn't matter, once his plan was completed, all would be set right.

All kinds of revelries had been arranged to celebrate the coming marriage and Grant thought they would never end, but at last, Ymirl and her women with all her golden gear, her jewels and valuable presents for the MacDonalds, were aboard ship. Sail was set for Scotland amid the tearful farewells and good wishes of all.

Grant was exultant, the skies were clear, the wind fair and the seas calm, the Fates were with him. Now he was sure he was meant to possess the fair maiden. Soon, soon she would be his.

Day after day they sailed on without problems. Although the sea was rough some days, there was none of the raging tempests that the North Sea could produce sending the ships and all aboard to the bottom.

Sometimes Ymirl, accompanied by one of her women, supped with the captain and Grant, but she gave no sign of any feelings for him. If he were disappointed, Grant did not show it.

At last they were within a day's voyage of the little bay close to the cave where Bonnie Prince Charlie landed on his return form Raasay. This bay is approximately 7 miles north of Portree where the ship was bound.

Grant had made a point of walking around the deck every night and standing talking with the helmsman for a while. That night he prepared to do the same thing, but before he went to talk to the helmsman, he looked carefully around the deck, and, seeing no one, he stopped in the shadows near the sail locker and spoke with two sailors lurking there.

"You know what to do and when to do it. You have sworn allegiance to me and I have sworn to reward you well. The time is come. Are you ready?"

"Aye, we're ready. You don't need to fear." Satisfied, Grant moved on to join the helmsman.

"All well?"

"Aye, Aye, Master."

They talked awhile as the ship sailed on through the night. There was no moon which suited Grant's plans well. There was a chill wind off the water and Grant pulled out a flask and took a drink. Then he offered it to the helmsman.

"It'll warm you," he said.

The helmsman took the flask gratefully, holding it to his mouth with one hand keeping the other on the helm. Grant stood close beside him, straining his eyes to see the light from the shore which was crucial to his plans. They had left Creag Mhor behind them and were in the narrow waters between the Isle of Sky and Raasay. Quickly, without any hesitation, Grant struck the helmsman a hard blow to the back of his neck with the edge of his hand.

Without a sound the man slipped on to the deck. Immediately, Grant took over the helm pushing the man to one side with his foot. Where was the light? Had the man forgotten? Had the ship arrived too soon or too late? Desperately he searched the dark line of the shore, the light should be dead ahead now he had changed course. But there was nothing, not the faintest glimmer of light.

Blood and Wounds! he muttered under his breath, was all to be lost by that old fool? He had gone too far to turn back now. He would have to find his way in by guess work. God's blood! I'll have his head when I get ashore. What could have happened? Douglas Moore was an old retainer of the family, he would never willingly betray him. But he was old and feeble. Could he be sick? Or simply have forgotten what to do? But no, he could not have forgotten because Grant had taken the precaution of telling him to put a light in the window of his bedchamber every night until Grant returned. Grant had never told him why, so Douglas could not betray him. He never knew that Grant intended to steer the ship on to the beach. Then in the confusion of darkness and wreck, he would make off with Ymirl. The two men he had sworn to secrecy would carry the chest of golden gear and the bags of gold and jewels, to the cave the three of them knew of. Then Grant intended to make his way with Ymirl, down the coast and get a ship to France. There he and Ymirl would live together forever.

Their families would believe they were both drowned in the wreck and their bodies carried away by the tides. If they were ever found out, Ymirl's father would never disclose the disgrace and dishonor of his daughter and the MacDonalds would die rather than reveal the treachery and villainy of one of their clan.

It was a perfect plan and it must succeed. It will, Grant determined as the little ship sailed on towards the phosphorescent waves breaking against the shore. Below, the Captain, crew and passengers were all asleep not dreaming of what was happening on deck. Not knowing that they would not live to see the dawn.

Suddenly, Grant saw the light. Twinkling and gleaming in the darkness, it was a beacon guiding him in. Thank God! Soon now, very soon, she will be mine, Grant thought his heart racing. What he didn't know was that Douglas Moore was dead. He had died of a rheum before Grant left Norway. The light was the lantern of a crofter watching over the difficult birthing of his one and only cow. And the lantern was four hundred yards beyond Douglas's home!

All unknowing, Grant steered on ready for the crash when the ship hit the beach. In the shadows the two sailors turned ready to grab the treasures and get safely away.

Now the phosphorent waves were only a hundred yards away, the light shone forth brightly and the little ship sailed on to its doom.

Too late, Grant caught the sound of waves against rocks. Too late, he realized he had missed the sandy beach. With a terrible splintering crash the ship hit the jagged rocks. The screams of the women mingled with the oaths of the crew as they struggled awake and tried to get on deck.

Grant leapt down to get Ymirl, shoving his way through the madly struggling bodies. Water was pouring in through a great gash in the hull. Grant caught a glimpse of Ymirl struggling to get through the water which was forcing her back against the bulkhead. Grant grasped her tightly and pulled her with him up to the hatch. Then, without warning, the ship listed as the bow dipped far into the water throwing them back with it.

Gasping for air, Grant tried to bring Ymirl to the surface, only to have her slip from his grasp. A foot touched his hand as he dived down to get her, but she was gone. Frantically he swam shouting her name, then with a tremendous shudder the ship settled down to the bottom as she slid off the rocks.

Grant had no chance to escape. He was crushed against the bulkhead and, like a squashed tomato his skull crumpled and his brains streamed out into the swirling waters.

Meanwhile the two men had not lost any time. They had brought up the treasure chests when Grant took the helm, so they were able to leap overboard before the ship struck. One was not a strong swimmer and, weighted down by bags of gold tied around his waist he had trouble getting ashore. His accomplice was strong and had no trouble with his load, but even he had as much as he could do to get to the beach.

He dropped the chest on the sand and sat beside it waiting for his companion. In a few moments he saw the shadowy shape crawling slowly towards him,

"I'm finished, Thomas, I canna do more. Take the stuff and leave me here."

"Don't give up, mon, rest a bit and ye'll be your self again. It was a hell of a trip and the stuff's heavy. He'd better be there when we get to the place."

"It's no good, I tell ye. I'm done for. Give me your hand. Look after my bairns for me."

Thomas bent down and took the man's hand. It was cold. His breathing was ragged and labored. Thomas knew he wouldn't last long. At any moment some might come in answer to the screaming from the ship and find them and treasure. Though this place was isolated, he knew there were a few crofter's around. Thomas took out his knife and cut the bags of gold from around the other man's waist and quickly tied them to his own belt.

"I'll best go on to the cave and when I've dumped the stuff, I'll be back for ye. I'll pull ye farther up from the water and if any find ye, they'll take ye for one of the shipwrecked."

Although he was so heavily laden, Thomas started up the cliff at a fair pace. Grant MacDonald had told them exactly where to hide the treasure and he climbed on without a backward look. He gave no thought to the ship or those aboard. He was sure that Grant MacDonald would have gotten off before the ship hit the rocks. And that was all he cared about. MacDonald had promised a very great reward and Thomas had no intention of losing it.

When Thomas saw that Grant was not in the cave, he sat down to wait after cutting off the bags of gold and pushing the treasure chest back in the depths of the cave. He was warm from the climb even though his clothes were wet. But after a while, the chill of the cave began to get to him. Cursing and muttering he got up and stamped around swinging his arms to warm himself. Soon it would be daylight. Where in God's Name was Grant MacDonald and the woman? If they didn't come soon he'd freeze to death waiting in this place.

He went further back in the cave but it was no warmer. He was afraid to leave. If I don't get paid off now, I never will, he thought. But I'm damned if I'm going to stay and turn stiff. He waited impatiently, expecting Grant to appear at any moment. He considered going part way down to meet Grant, but he was afraid to leave the treasure lying around in the cave, Grant would kill him if any were lost or if he didn't follow his orders exactly. There was nothing for it, but to wait.

Hour after hour passed. He waited through the night and through the next day until night fell again. Then his anger gave way to fear. Something must have gone wrong. He'd been told that Ymirl was being forced to marry Donald MacDonald even though she was secretly married to someone else and Grant was helping her escape to the husband she loved.

The treasure belonged to her and that is why it had to be safe and taken to the cave so that the Lady Ymirl could go to her husband with a proper dowry. Grant had promised Thomas and his accomplice that they would be paid with more gold than they could earn in a lifetime. Now Thomas was wondering what would happen to him if Grant MacDonald's plans had been discovered.

What would they say of him? Would Thomas and his partner be blamed for everything? That's what the nobles always did. They put the blame on the poor and left them to pay the price.

Finally, Thomas decided to get out. He'd had no food or water for twenty four hours and he was chilled to the bone. Before he left he took the treasure and the bags of gold as far back in the cave as he could get. Then he pushed the bags under a crevice and put stones and dust from the floor all over and in front of them so that it would not show any signs of being disturbed. Then he shoved the chest behind a protruding piece of rock, hacking at it with a stone until some portions fell over it.

Then he started down the hill. His knees were shaking and he made slow progress, but eventually he reached the shore. He made sure there was no one about before he came into the open. Even though he walked over the whole stretch of beach, he found no trace of his friend.

He was not too worried because he considered that from the look of things, the wreck had been discovered and anyone alive would have been taken in by the crofters and bodies would be taken to the church to await burial. So, Thomas started off towards the light he could see in the distance. He was desperate for food and water and he wanted to find out how the land lay. He had to do something. He was starving and almost frozen by the bitter wind that blew in off the sea.

Thomas was not to know that the light was the very same lantern that had brought the ship on to the rocks. The crofter, a dour, youngish man, took him inside the cottage where a warm fire was burning on the hearth.

"Warm yerself, mon, and I'll give ye some porage. That'll bring the life back into ye. Where've ye been since the night? All the rest were brought in this morning."

Seated on the rough bench before the fire, Thomas began to feel a bit stronger.

"I must have been near drowned, but when I came to, I was washed up on the beach behind some rocks there. I've been wandering around looking for my shipmates. Then I saw your light and made for it."

"It was a bad night for all aboard. There was only one of the puir things left alive, they say and 'tis said the nephew of the MacDonald himself was found dead along with the noble lady who was to marry with MacDonald's son."

"Dead! you say he's dead the MacDonald's nephew is dead?"

"Aye, and the lady. Though Grant MacDonald's head was all smashed in they knew him by his fine clothes and his ring that was still on his finger. They've sent to tell the MacDonald. Sad news for him, I fear."

Thomas was silent thinking about his money. He would never get it now. What should he do about the gold and treasure? Could he keep it for himself? No, he dare not. The lady Ymirl's husband and the MacDonalds would be searching for it. The shore would be crawling with people not only MacDonalds but their enemies the MacLeods all looking for the golden gear when once the news got around. Thomas knew he'd better keep quiet and make himself scarce. And that's exactly what he did.

Thomas signed on with another ship and never told a soul about the gold or treasure until he lay dying. Then he told the woman who was looking after him. She went to look for the treasure with her brother but they never found the cave and so they thought Thomas was wandering in his mind and made it all up.

Off and on others have gone searching, but so far none have found it. But it would make a wonderful vacation to go and stay in these parts and go over the hills with a metal detector and look for the cave. The scenery is beautiful and the natives friendly and you might come back far richer than you went.

Calve Island
Tobermory
Sound of Mull
Ulva
MULL
To oban
Duart Castle
Ben More
Ross of Mull
Firth of Lorn
0
5
10

Notes on the MacDonald Gold

Broadford Village, not far from Portree, has a great cairn on top of the hill of Bienn no Callich under which a Norwegian princess is buried. Whether this is Ymirl's final resting place, no one knows, but it very well could be.

Around this same area there are other treasures waiting to be found. When Francis Drake defeated the Spanish Armada, the galleons fled north hoping to sail around Scotland and then back to Spain. A great storm arose and the fleet was scattered, many galleons were wrecked on the rocky coastline.

One galleon is said to lie in *Staffin Bay,* which is on the east coast of the Tratternish area of Skye. Gold coins have been found on the shore from time to time which supports this story.

The people of Staffin are of spanish descent and claim to be offspring of the sailors saved from the wreck.

The Island of Fladda-chelain has a ruined chapel which is named for St. Columba. This chapel has an altar made of local blue stone and has the power of bringing fair winds to becalmed ships if the right prayers are said. It is in this little church that Sir Donald MacDonald hid the title deeds of the Isles when he left to take part in the battle of Culloden in 1745.

South of Sky is the *Island of Mull* and the beautiful harbor of *Tobermory* made famous by the Duke of Argyle's search for the treasure lost when the Spanish galleon Almirante de Florencia was wrecked in 1588.

This ship from the defeated Armada anchored in the bay to get provisions. Stores of all kinds were provided by the people, but the Spaniards did not pay. They kept promising to pay on another day. When the people saw the galleon being readied to leave they asked their Laird, Donald McLean, to try and get their money for them.

McLean went on board to get what was owing but, instead of handing over the money, the Spanish seized and imprisoned him. Somehow, McLean managed to escape and reach the magazine. Then he blew up the ship killing almost all on board. A few escaped and the officers were thrown into Duart Castle and kept imprisoned.

The Almirante de Florencia was carrying treasure of fifty million ducats when it was sunk. However, the navy divers, who were diving for the Duke of Argyle, found only a few gold coins. Many believe the treasure is still there, but others think the Governor of the Isle of Man may have found the treasure when he sent divers down in 1688.

Duart Castle, the ancestral home of the McLeans had been beautifully restored by the family. The 27th chief of the clan McLean now opens the castle to the public.

The Duart museum is well worth a visit. It has many relics of the MacLean family and also a rare collection of Scottish Boy Scout history.

The MacLeans were at one time supporters of the MacDougalls and then they later gave their allegiance to the Lords of the Isles, the MacDougals.

In the sixteenth and seventeenth centuries, the MacLeans were of great importance in the Western Isles. They were brave and fearless fighters and, in the battle of InverKeithing seven MacLean brothers gave their lives to protect their chief. One after another they fought to the death, shouting as they fell, "Another for Hector." In spite of their bravery their chief, Sir Hector MacLean was killed. This story is a constant source of inspiration to the clan.

The Clan MacLean has its own organization with headquarters in Glasgow.

SANDY ROBERTSON AND THE SOLID GOLD CAT.

Sandy Robertson and the Solid Gold Cat

by P.B. Innis

When I first saw Alexander Robertson, (Sandy for short), he was walking across the lobby of the Gotham Hotel in New York. I was thirty years old at the time and thought highly of myself, disillusionment had not yet set in. But I had never imagined anyone could be quite as self assured as the man in the lobby.

He was of medium height, of slender build and dressed in a Scottish kilt with all accompanying regalia including a dirk in his sock. His hair under his bonnet was reddish gold and his eyes a surprising brown instead of the expected blue-grey. All this was unusual enough but, if you can believe it, he was leading a marmalade cat on a matching leash! Both walked across that lobby as if they owned it.

I was fascinated. I could not take my eyes of them. I had to know more, so I followed them into the elevator and thence to a room full of persons attired in a similar tartan. I recognized it at once. Robertson! It must be a Robertson Clan meeting or some such thing.

With some trepidation I walked to the bar and picked up a drink. Being an Innis, I was not sure how the Robertsons would welcome me. But I need not have worried, they accepted me without question merely saying,

"Get yourself a kilt, mon."

It was obvious from the way they greeted them, that the man and the cat were well known to the Robertsons. They showed no surprise at their appearance, nor seemed to mind the animal's presence. A Robertson cat, I assumed.

I walked over and a cheerful looking Robertson with a large nameplate saying, Hello, I'm Randy, put out his hand and said,

"Hello, I'm Randy"

"Hello, I'm P.B." I answered.

Glad to know you, PeeBee. Do'ye know Sandy here?" and he introduced me to the cat man.

"Alexander Robertson at your service. Meet Bastet," and he looked down at the cat who stared back at me with large, round, impervious eyes.

"How do you do Basket." I said politely, not daring to try and stroke the dignified creature. "I've always liked marmalade cats."

"Marmalade! I must rebuke you, sir, Bastet is a Golden Cat directly descended from the Gods of the Pharoahs of Egypt."

"Forgive me." I said, feeling suitably rebuked. "I haven't met such a cat before."

"That cat's not only a Golden Cat, but it thinks it's God Himself." Randy interjected trying to be helpful.

"It seems to me that Mr. PeeBee is ignorant of the Gods of Egypt. Bastet, I'll have you know, was the Goddess of Happiness, known as the Cat God. This animal's ancestors lived in a sacred compound. People begged them to intercede with the Cat Goddess on their behalf. The mummies of Bastet's ancestors are still to be found in the tombs of Kings. This animal must be treated with respect."

Sandy pronounced this with such awful emphasis that it produced a horrible silence as all the Robertsons turned to see what was going on. Nervously, looking for the door, I said,

"I'm glad to learn all this about your cat and I will make absolutely sure that I always treat, Basket, the Golden Cat, with proper respect should we meet in the future."

"I thankyou on Bastet's behalf and you may consider your oversight forgiven."

"Thankyou," I murmured, wondering vaguely whether the man was completely crazy, putting on an act or what.

Seeing that nothing was about to happen the Robertsons went back to their drinking and conviviality. I was making for the door when Randy said,

Have another dram before you leave. It'll settle your nerves." and he introduced me to Douglas, a huge Robertson who took me around the room fully convinced I was a longlost cousin.

Later, I had a chance to talk with Randy and found out that he considered Sandy was one of the best Robertsons in the Clan.

"He comes to all the functions and he contributes generously. Mind you, I don't believe that orange cat is any goddess, but I go along with him. To my mind, Sandy brings something interesting to the meetings. He's good for morale. He knows more about the Robertsons than all the rest of us put together. Everyone likes to be told their ancestors are the cat's whiskers, even if they are not gods."

"Is he really Scottish?"

"Of course he is. Can't you tell by the way he talks?"

"Well. Yes. I suppose so." Secretly I thought his accent was phony. A mixture of Brooklynese and stage Scottish, but, perhaps he had been in the States so long that he had lost his original speech. "Why does he call the cat Basket. It's a strange name for a cat."

"It's Bastet not Basket. It's written with two ts not a k. You can see it on that thing around its neck."

Bastette sounds even worse. Seems like a female bastard."

Randy laughed,

"You'd better be careful. Sandy's very touchy about that cat. Bastet was some kind of Egyptian Goddess and he really believes it."

"What does he do for a living?"

"He's an investor and real estate man. He has land in Scotland and also over here."

"Well, he's certainly an interesting personality." I said, watching Sandy as he and the cat worked the room.

Hoping I would see them again, I wished Sandy and Bastet "Goodnight" and went home. I was taking an early flight to Washington the next day, so I didn't want to be too late getting to bed.

When I got back from Washington, there was a note from Sandy inviting me for a drink with him and Bastet at a little bar close by.

"I thought ye needed to know more about the gods and goddesses of old." he said, "Ye can't be a good Robertson and not know about the Golden Cat."

I realized that I was with him on false pretenses and must put things right before it was too late.

"I'm not really a Robertson, Sandy, I'm an Innis. I was with you the other night by mistake."

"Mistake, mon! What do ye mean? Either you're a Robertson or ye're not and it ye're an Innis ye're not a Robertson now, are ye?"

"No, I'm not. I'm sorry I misled you. Why don't you let me buy the drinks."

"Nay, I'll not let ye. I asked ye and so I'll pay. But mind ye, I'll have no more mistakes." Then his face brightened, "Innis is a guid Scottish name and ye must be a guid Scotch man. After all, we can't all be Robertsons now, can we?"

"No, I suppose not. But tell me about the Golden Cat and how its mixed up with the Robertsons. I've never heard of it 'til now."

"Well, there's a lot of things in this world ye might not have heard of, but that doesn't men they're not there now, does it?"

"No, of course not." I said irritated with the man. I hated to be talked down to or have it suggested that I didn't know much.

"Guid, guid, now ye're mind's ready to take in what I'm going to tell ye." And Sandy leant over the table towards me and started his tale.

"Now, laddie, some will tell ye that the Robertsons are descended from the Earls of Atholl and got their Clan name of Donnachadh from Donnachadh who led the clan in the great Battle of Bannockburn and was a good friend of King Robert Bruce. We got the name of Robertson from Robert Riach the great chief who captured the murdering assassins of King James 1st. The Robertsons fought loyally for the Stuarts and were handsomely rewarded even to getting a naked, manacled man added to their Arms, but, through the devilish plans of their enemies, they lost most of their lands."

"This is all very interesting, but where does the marm- the golden Cat come in?" I was getting impatient. I didn't want the whole history of the Robertsons, just the cat.

"Be patient, Laddie, I'm coming to that. Now, while all the above is true, there's more to the Robertsons than that. They are much older than any other clan. They were old before the Picts or the Scots were heard of. They started out from Alexandria, Egypt. That's why many of them are called Alexander like me. From Alexandria they went to Persia and Sicily, Normandy, South West Britain, then up to the Isles. Some of them even went to Iceland and then America and they brought with them the Golden Cats."

Sandy paused for effect, then went on, "these cats were their mascot and brought good luck and good fortune because they belonged to the Cat Goddess. Those early Robertsons made their money breeding Golden Cats and selling them to people for mascots." Sandy paused again, "Now, listen carefully laddie, their own mascot was a foot high cat made of solid gold. Solid gold, laddie, think of that. This cat was kept by the chief and was where he got his power. Then about 1100 the cat disappeared and nobody's seen it since. I, Alexander Robertson am the true chief of the Robertsons and would be now, only a whole lot of bastards got in the way. But, when I find the golden mascot they will recognize me as the chief and I'll claim my rights."

Sandy paused for breath and I took the chance to ask,

"Have you any idea where the Golden Cat might be?"

"Yes, Laddie, I have. I consider I know where to set my hand on it, but its a difficult and expensive job and this is where you come in. I'll let you invest in my search and you will be handsomely rewarded when I come into my own. What do you say? $5,000-$500, anything you can spare."

Now I understood. It was all a racket. Sandy was just another con artist.

"Sorry, I don't have any money to throw away on a racket like this." I said getting up from the table and letting him know what I thought of his scheme.

Indignantly, Sandy raised his voice, "Racket! you insult me. This is no racket, I can prove everything I say."

"Save your breath, I'm not interested." I said coldly and walked out. Later I remembered the hurt look on his face when I called him a con artist. Well, he'd asked for it, I thought, I knew he was a phony right from the start. Hadn't he called a Scotsman, Scotch, which no true Scotsman would do, and everyone knew the Robertsons did not come from Egypt.

Disappointed and feeling badly let down, I didn't go back to the Robertson meeting place for some time. Then one morning I opened the paper and saw Sandy and the Cat looking at me.

SCOTSMAN SUED FOR OBTAINING MONEY ON FALSE PRETENSES

Reading through the piece I saw that Sandy had collected $250 from a number of people who thought they were buying a piece of land on Ben Nevis. When they received a small bag containing an ounce or two of what Sandy called, Soil of the land of their ancestors, they complained bitterly and two of them sued.

Selling Ben Nevis is like selling the Brooklyn Bridge and I had to admire Sandy's salesmanship. Evidently, he had done better with this racket than he had with his search for the Golden Cat.

Anxious to know more I called Randy who told me the whole thing was a mistake. Sandy had offered people some Scottish soil and he had provided it. It would have cost them much more to go to Scotland and dig up their own dirt.

The case was dismissed and Sandy was back in business again, but I didn't see him until Randy invited me to a gathering of the Association of Athol-men. This organization is made up of Stewarts of Atholl and Robertsons. There in all his glory was Sandy and Golden Cat.

This time Sandy was in full dress and really looked grand. He greeted me civilly but there was still that hurt look in his eye as he said,

"I expected better things from an Innis."

Somehow he made me feel like a Judas. I stooped down to stroke Bastet, but hastily withdrew when I saw the hair rise on her neck and heard her warning snarl.

After this I left New York but, off and on, I heard tell of Sandy and the Golden Cat. They were still selling their Scottish soil, appearing at Scottish Events and, I assumed, searching for the solid gold Feline. Everywhere Sandy went, he proudly proclaimed the wonders of his Robertson ancestry.

As the years went by I forgot them, though occasionally, I'd see a marmalade cat and it reminded me of them.

Then, one day, I was walking down Connecticut Avenue in Washington D.C. when I saw in the distance a tartan clad figure leading a dishevelled looking cat. It was Sandy!! But not the Sandy of old. This was an old, fragile looking man clad in a frayed kilt. His shoes were cracked and broken, his shirt was clean, but had been haphazardly mended and his bonnet was battered out of shape.

The Golden Cat was skinny instead of sleek and plump. Strands of black protruded from the gold hairs. It was evident they had fallen on evil days.

"Sandy, is it really you." I found myself glad to see him and upset about his shabby, pathetic appearance.

At first he didn't seem to recognize me, then pulling himself up with his old dignity he said,

"Yes, it is I, Alexander Robertson and Bastet at your service, sir."

"I'm glad to see you, Sandy, why don't we go somewhere we can talk. We can have a drink or something." I added hastily, he looked in need of a good meal.

Sandy hesitated, and then he said,

"Our investments have not done well lately. I am not in a position to entertain you."

"But its my turn, Sandy, the last time we were together you paid the bills, don't you remember? Its been on my conscience and I'd like to pay you back."

"Well, in that case, perhaps a wee drop of whiskey—" his voice gained strength at the thought.

"Of course, but I haven't had lunch yet. I hope you'll join me and eat something first."

"I'd be glad to, laddie. Let's see now, its a good many years since we last met."

"It certainly is. It was at the Gathering of Atholl-men and you looked very grand."

A sad smile crept across his face,

"They were guid days, guid days—then."

I took him to Howard Johnson as that was the nearest and we sat in a secluded corner where Bastet would not be noticed. I had a momentary embarrassment at being seen with such a shabby person, but, thank God, the years had knocked some humility into me and I no longer judged people as critically as I used to do.

Seeing the dignified way Sandy and Cat behaved towards me in spite of their obvious poverty, I felt ashamed of my past behavior towards them.

"What would you like?" I asked, handing him the menu.

"Would you order for me, laddie, Me and Bastet can enjoy anything that's set before us."

When the food arrived he surreptitiously poured some cream into his saucer, crumbled some bread in it and gave it to Bastet. Then he started to eat. I noticed how his hand shook as he picked up his fork.

"I am sorry to hear that your investments have not done so well lately. How is your search for the solid Gold Cat?"

Unfortunately, it has not proved possible to get people to invest the necessary money for me to go and get it. People are very unbelieving nowadays."

He was too polite to refer to my rejection and I did not mention it either.

I hope you are doing well, laddie, you always intended to get on in the world."

"I haven't done too badly. But tell me, have you seen or heard anything of Randy? I've often wondered about him."

"Randy, puir Randy, he died five years ago. I was very upset. Too upset to do anything about my investments. Also, at that time, Bastet, the Golden Cat you used to know, died of old age. She was nineteen, very old for a cat. This Bastet is her child, but she is not the equal of her mother. As you can see, she is not pure gold. Her mother must have forgotton her pedigree and coupled with an ordinary cat. I fear that it was not a good omen, but I try to keep hopeful that I will succeed in finding the solid Gold Cat and claiming what is mine."

I hope you do." and indeed I did most fervently. There was something about this pair that touched me deeply. They did not bow to adversity but they were badly bent by it. Bravely they kept fighting.

"If you would allow me, I would like to invest in your search on the understanding that you give me a share when you find the solid Gold Cat and come into your own." I was careful not to hurt his feelings by offering charity.

"I will be glad to let you in on my plan, but I cannot promise success in any given time. Would you be able to wait?"

"Oh, yes, of course, I know how long these things can take. They are quite unpredictable. I was thinking about $500 or so. Would that be acceptable?"

"Certainly, and I will give you a receipt."

I gave him the money later that day and he gave me a receipt. Somehow he had obtained a piece of paper and had written it out quite formally.

I never saw him again, but the picture of that shabby figure walking carefully along the street leading the sadly dishevelled, partly Golden Cat, has stayed in my mind. I am thankful I saved my conscience with a little money. Especially as I came across an article the other day showing how the orange cats all came westward from Egypt, probably by sea. The map see page 64 shows they followed the route Sandy described, bypassing Ireland going up to the Hebrides and on to Iceland.

Sandy could never have seen this article. He had told the tale long before it was written. Was his tale true after all? Was there a solid Gold Cat of the Robertsons? Did Sandy ever find it. I'm afraid I'll never know.

Map shows route the orange cats travelled from Egypt. Probably hopping aboard ships. Scientific America, 281, 1977, has an article on this by Neil B. Todd.

THE CACHE OF THE CLAN MACGREGOR

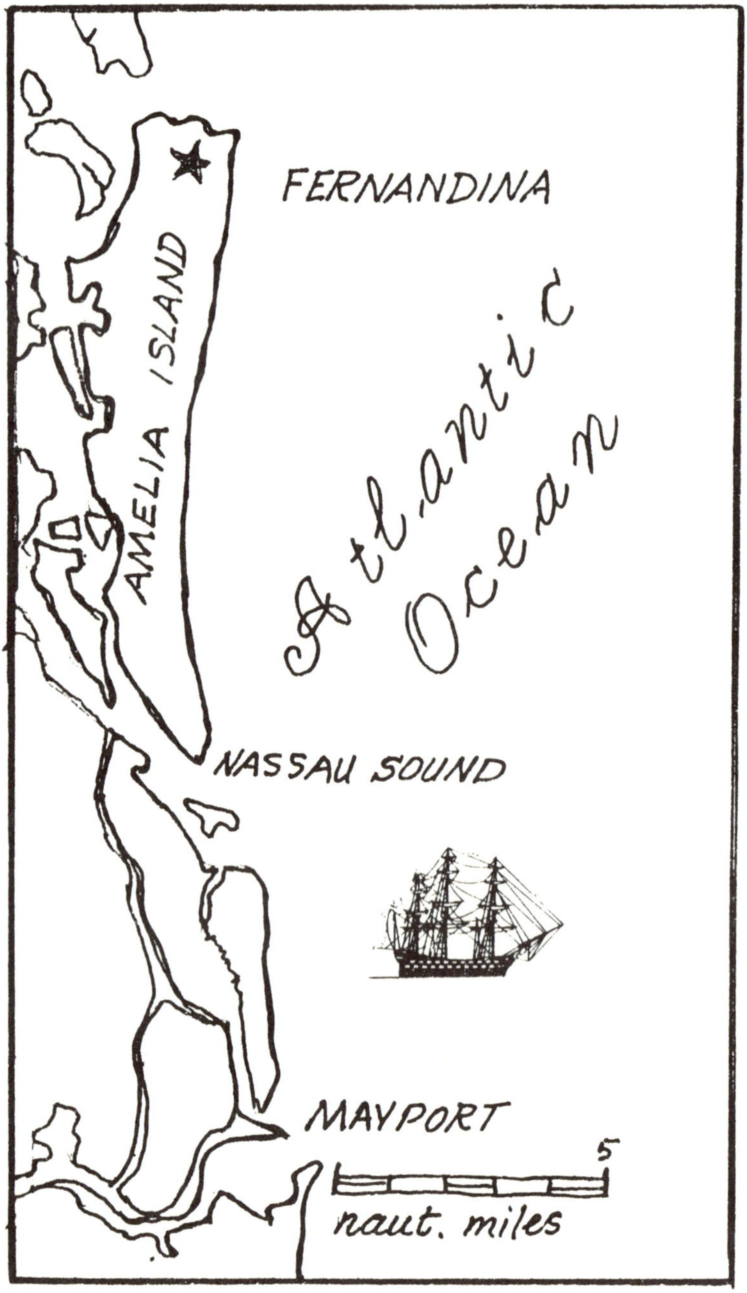
FERNANDINA
AMELIA ISLAND
Atlantic Ocean
NASSAU SOUND
MAYPORT
5
naut. miles

The Cache of the Clan MacGregor

The best known MacGregor is probably Rob Roy, the MacGregor whose adventures and persecutions were made famous by Sir Walter Scott. But there are many other MacGregors who led equally roistering, adventurous lives and who were constantly on the run from their many enemies.

This meant that they often had to leave their lairs in a hurry and hide their valuables as best as they could, taking the chance that they would live to return and retrieve them. Consequently, there are tales of several MacGregor treasure caches that have never been collected. The two that seemed to us the most credible are described in the following pages. One is in the Highlands of Scotland and one in Florida.

Most historians agree that the MacGregors are one of the purest and oldest of the Celtic tribes. Their ancient motto is "My race is royal." This comes from an early ancestor, Griogar who was the third son of King Alpin of Scotland who reigned in the ninth century.

While Glenurchy was the original home of the MacGregors, at the height of their power they possessed vast lands in Perthshire, Argyleshire, Glenstrae, Glengyle and Glenlyon. These lands were acquired by "right of first possession" (squatter's rights). The MacGregors held the lands by "right of the sword" but, because they did not bother about title deeds, their enemies, the Campbells were able to secretly and by the most devious means, get Crown Charters to much of the MacGregor land. Then they tried to force the MacGregors off and take possession themselves. But the MacGregors held on to the lands they considered were rightfully theirs, fighting off the Campbells again and again. In spite of their fierce attempts to keep out the Campbells, the MacGregors were eventually overcome and expelled from the lands they had occupied for centuries. The proud MacGregors were in the situation of being tenants where once they had ruled with absolute power.

Bitterly hostile and aggressive the MacGregors began harassing the Campbells every way they could. Because they now had no means of subsistence the MacGregor clan was forced to rob and steal from their oppressors. Considering what they took as rightfully theirs, the MacGregors attacked the Campbells and the Campbell allies whenever and wherever they could. This made it possible for the Campbells to complain to the King that unless the MacGregor Clan was cut off root and branch, there would never be any peace in Scotland.

The MacGregors were outlawed, then commissions were formed to pursue them with fire and sword. The Chief of MacGregor was deprived of his last remaining land by an Act of Parliament in 1563. In 1603 an Act was passed taking from the MacGregors the right to use their own name and they were forced to swear that their bairns already born and those that might be born in some future time would not bear the name of MacGregor. The penalty for disobeying this order was execution without trial.

After this Act, members of the Clan took various other names, but they never bowed their heads to their oppressors. They fled to the hills and hid out in the mountains and continued their plunderings from there.

Some people ask why the MacGregors allowed the Campbells to get charters to their lands. Why didn't they get the charters themselves? Americans will easily understand the MacGregors because of similar happenings in this country's early days. Land was settled by people who claimed it by "right of first occupancy." They were there first so it was theirs. They built their house after clearing the land and cultivated as much as they could. There was no way and no need to register their claims in the early days of the West and, by the time more and more settlers came in and Land Offices were registering claims, the early settlers often thought it unnecessary to go and register their land as everyone knew they lived there. Unscrupulous land dealers would look up desirable tracts to see if a claim was registered and, if not, they would make a claim and the original settlers would be forced out.

The case of Daniel Boone is a good example. Daniel lost all his lands in Kentucky because he failed to register them and he was turned off them by someone who had gone behind his back and had them surveyed and registered in his name.

By the middle of the seventeenth century, the MacGregors could not sign any document with their name, no agreement made with a MacGregor was legal, no Minister was allowed to baptize their children and they could be killed by anyone without fear of punishment by the Law.

Rob Roy was the son of the MacGregor of Glengyle. He took the name of Campbell but was usually known as RED ROB. In 1624 the Earl of Moray brought some 300 MacGregors to his estates in Mentieth to help him fight against the Mackintoshes. Rob Roy obtained some lands called Craig Royston and married the daughter of MacGregor of Cromar. Rob Roy was a trader in cattle and needing money to increase his stock, he borrowed from the Duke of Montrose. Unfortunately, he was unable to repay this loan and, fearing the Duke's anger, he fled. The Duke prosecuted him and some law officers who went searching for Rob Roy found only his wife. They treated her shamefully and this so angered Rob Roy that his whole temperament was changed.

The Duke took Rob Roy's lands and Rob Roy became an outlaw. He gathered a band of men who shared his hatred of the oppressors of the MacGregors and until Rob Roy died, they helped themselves to the cattle and other produce of the Duke's Estate. They never took from the tenants, only that which belonged to the Duke. All their plunderings were made in broad daylight in spite of all that the Duke tried to do to stop them.

Towards the end of his life, Rob Roy was back at Royston and it is here that he is said to have cached away much of the gold he had collected.

Craig Royston is on the east side of Loch Lomond. It is a rocky wooded area and as there is no map or clue showing where the cache was hidden, the only way to find it would be to cover the ground with a metal detector. There are several deep indentures in the rock which would make a good hiding place for bags of gold. The gold is said to be contained in skin bags. Around this area there must be many metal pieces of historical value as well as the cache of gold. Although the MacGregors were reduced to poverty, they still had the rich badges and buckles and swords of their inheritance. A treasure hunt here would be well worthwhile.

In spite of their cruel sufferings and oppressions, the MacGregors remained faithful to the Jacobite cause fighting bravely on the side of the King. Charles the II was so grateful to the MacGregors for their support that he repealed the Act against them and "wiped off all memory of their Miscarriages and took off all mark of reproach." However, this did not last long. William of Orange took their rights again and it was not until William Adam, M.P. introduced a Bill into Parliament in 1775 to restore the rights and immunities of the Clan MacGregor, that they once more came into some part of their own.

MacGregors are not the kind to sit around doing nothing and many emigrated to America, many served their country in various wars overseas. One very interesting character left a fortune hidden off the coast of Florida and, as far as we know, never came back to claim it.

In the years after the war of 1812, Florida was held by the Spanish, but was ardently desired by the Americans. Also, it was feared that the British might try and take it back at any time. The Spanish had their hands full with trouble at home and in Latin America and so their hold on Florida was very weak. Knowing this, all kinds of adventurers were promoting revolutionary movements in Florida.

Among these was Gregor MacGregor who landed in Fernandina on June 29 1817. MacGregor landed in the name of the Republics of Venezuela, New Granada, Rio de la Plata and Mexico. MacGregor had been fighting with the British in the Napoleonic wars in Europe and had then gone to South America and fought with Bolivar and Miranda to free Venezuela. However, he found he did not want to settle there and so sailed on to Baltimore.

In Baltimore MacGregor visited many Americans and got promises of support from them in return for promises of land in Florida when he took that area. Then he went on to Charleston and Savannah soliciting supplies. MacGregor had no difficulty in getting these and he also managed to raise an armed force from the veterans of the 1812 war to go with him to Fernandina.

MacGregor assembled his army at the mouth of the Altamaha river sending ahead messages of his advance and enormous supply of men and ships as well as guns and ammunition. Such a display of confidence dismayed the Spanish so that when MacGregor reached Fernandina, the Spanish garrison surrendered without firing a shot.

Elated with victory, MacGregor raised the shortest lived flag that ever flew over Florida, a green cross of St. George on a white field. This came to be known as the Green Cross of Florida.

The promised aid from Florida never arrived to MacGregor's great disgust, but, on August the 28th, the High Sheriff of New York

City, one Ruggles Hubbard, arrived on a ship called the Morgiana. Ruggles encouraged MacGregor to believe that all kinds of aid was forthcoming and, on the strength of this, MacGregor declared a blockade of the coast of Florida from Amelia Island to the Perdido River.

On September 4, the Spanish, realizing that something had to be done, launched an attack from St. Augustine. MacGregor, having no desire to take on Spain, decided to sail away and leave the affair in the hands of Hubbard. MacGregor gave Hubbard authority to use all the supplies including the gold which had been collected for the revolution, to fight the Spanish.

The Spanish attack failed completely, this was not because of Hubbard's efforts but because of Spanish bad management. Hubbard made great plans for festivities to be held in Fernandina, but, before the victory could be celebrated with any vigor, the pirate, Luis Autry arrived and opened fire on the town.

Taken by surprise, Hubbard was forced to surrender and Autry raised the flag of Mexico over Fernandina. Two of MacGregors faithful followers tried to escape with the gold, but their little boat was spotted and sunk by pirate fire just off the coast. The gold went down with them and is probably still sunk into the sand not far from the shore.

The map on page 66 gives the area and probable site of the lost gold.

Has anyone found it? Not that we have heard. But we know that Gregor MacGregor of MacGregor has recently bought a place on Key Largo and spends part of the year there. Does he go up to Fernandina seeking his ancestor's gold? Is this why he spends part of the year in Florida and the rest at his home in Scotland?

We have been wondering, but, so far, we haven't dared to ask!!

PIPER — THE BLACK WATCH REGIMENT.

MACGREGOR'S CIPHER.

MacGregor's Cipher

During the Revolutionary war, a Mrs. Gordon ran a comfortable boarding house in Front Street Philadelphia. This boarding house was chiefly occupied by British Officers who appreciated Mrs. Gordon's good cooking. Among those who stayed at Mrs. Gordon's was a Captain Reid who had a servant called MacGregor.

Both Reid and MacGregor were very popular as Captain Reid composed music and MacGregor had a good voice and would sing the scottish songs Captain Reid played on his flute.

At this time Philadelphia was in the hands of the British who had taken it peacefully after the Battle of Brandywine. MacGregor, a cheerful, gregarious man, quickly made friends with an easy going, pretty little kitchen maid named Rosa.

Rosa took a great fancy to MacGregor who successfully wooed her with Scottish Ballads sung in his mellow tenor. Rosa's father had been a soldier in the Royal Highland Regiment, known as the 42nd. He had married her mother, a Scottish immigrant, just before he was killed in action.

Rosa's mother had supported them both until she died of fever when Rosa was fourteen years old. Rosa, who by now, had no illusions about life, went to work for Mrs. Gordon and when she met MacGregor, she had been there for the past four years.

When MacGregor became more and more passionate, Rosa began to withdraw a little. Did he want to make an honest woman of her? Or was he like all the rest, out for what he could get?

MacGregor swore undying devotion and that he sorely wanted to make her his wife. But, when Rosa wanted to set the day, he wouldn't be pinned down.

Mrs. Gordon, who took a motherly interest in Rosa, spoke to MacGregor in no uncertain terms.

"Either marry her, or leave her alone." Poor MacGregor saw there was nothing for it but to confess that he already had a wife.

"I thought as much," said Mrs. Gordon bitterly. "You men are all alike. Deceiving a poor, friendless and helpless orphan girl, just for your own pleasure. Get out of here and never darken my door again."

MacGregor was about to slink out without a word to Rosa, but she, knowing that Mrs. Gordon was going to confront him, was anxiously awaiting results outside the door.

"Tell her the truth," Mrs. Gordon shouted. "Tell her you've a wife already."

Flabbergasted, poor Rosa shrieked,

"I don't believe it. Ye wouldn't deceive me, would ye?"

Wishing he were anywhere but Mrs. Gordon's boarding house, MacGregor admitted his guilt. Whereupon Rosa, her red hair falling down her back, smote him on the top of his head with the iron kettle she had been cleaning.

MacGregor fell like a stone.

"My God! You've killed him, girl. Go! Get the Captain quickly."

Rosa fled to the Captain's door who, hearing the noise was already coming out to see what was going on. He saw at once that MacGregor was badly hurt and sent for the surgeon.

For days MacGregor lay at death's door, not moving an eyelid. Poor, heartbroken Rosa hovered over him praying that he wouldn't die.

At last MacGregor opened his eyes which were still slightly crossed from the blow, looked at Rosa and smiled.

With tears dropping on the sheets, Rosa knelt at the bedside begging forgiveness.

"I never meant to hurt ye," she sobbed. "Not that bad even though ye did deceive me so."

"You never hurt me, lass. But tell me how did I get here and what's wrong with me head?" MacGregor had no recollection of what had happened.

"It's a good thing you've got a wooden head. That's all I can say." Mrs. Gordon sniffed.

MacGregor recovered slowly, but the Captain had to move on without him. MacGregor was never quite the same again, but he did rejoin the regiment later.

Rosa confessed that it was she who conked him on the head, but she loved him and said she would always take care of him. MacGregor said he would never go back to England, so she was as good as his wife. They spent as much time together as his regiment's movements would allow and kept in touch in between with letters written in MacGregor's special cipher.

Rosa remained reasonably faithful and, when MacGregor, who was much older than she, died, he left her all his possessions.

His Will like his letters, was written in the cipher. Below is a message written in this cipher. Can you read it?

A knowledge of Scottish regimental songs is useful.

7.16.65.62.120.58.72.24.90.192.192.62.150.146.
155.109.131.106.139.168.139.72.195.184.122.20.6.
72.195.159.192.57.164.168.170.58.68.117.1-22.44.70.80.
142.72.131.153.127.62.153.192.70.158.174.49.106.1-179.
163.146.1-102.57.75.169.103.178.78.192.162.133.144.4.
58.65.90.78.146.116.1-106.15.146.139.146.101.1-173.
158.153.171.

THE JEWELLED CROSS OF BLACK ISLE.

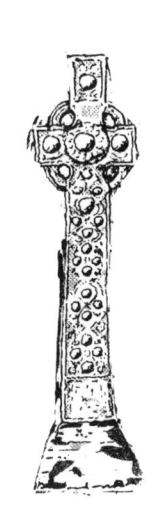

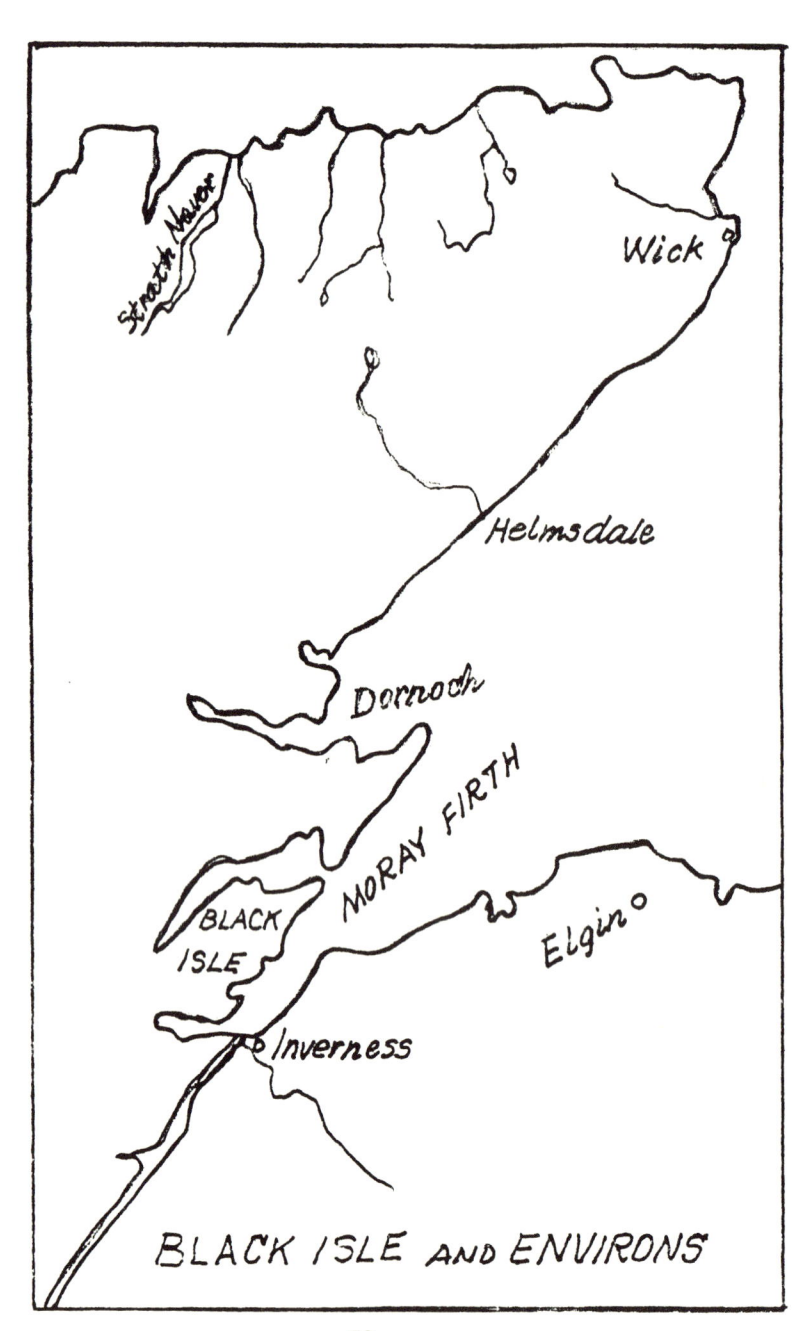

BLACK ISLE AND ENVIRONS

The Jewelled Cross
of the Black Isle

The dark ruins of the castle were outlined against the setting sun. They were all that was left of a once splendid stronghold. The land around was equally desolate. Once sheep and cattle had grazed here and the place had echoed with the sounds of everyday living. Now, all was silent. The savagery of the battle that had raged around the castle had left such a gruesome aura that not even a bird flew near.

The sun sank lower and one of the dying rays caught the crumbling parapet and showed a figure standing there. The man was looking straight into the sunset, his tattered plaid wrapped tightly around his body making him look taller than he really was. The sun sank lower and the blood red rays caught the horrible, mutilated stumps of the man's arms so that they looked as bloody as the day his hands were hacked off by the brother of his bride to be.

Ralston Munro hated mankind with a savage bitterness that devoured his every thought. He lived for only one thing and that was revenge. Revenge kept him alive. Revenge enabled him to survive inhuman suffering, loneliness, despair and starvation. Revenge was all that was left to him. Every night he came to watch the setting sun and renew his vow of revenge.

Every night as the sun set, he would turn and go back into the silence and darkness of the ruined castle for this was his only home.

Ten years earlier, Munro had been a handsome daredevil of twenty six, capable of outriding and outfighting anyone. He was betrothed to Jean, daughter of Ian Stewart. Although Munro was a younger son, he had sufficient lands of his own which he had inherited from his mother, to live very well and independently.

Ralston and Jean's brother, Andrew, were fast friends, so that when some of Andrew's cattle were driven off by a band of outlaws, Ralston raised thirty men to help Andrew get them back.

Each at the head of his own men, Ralston and Andrew rode through the night intending to catch up with the thieves and take them by surprise. Luck was with them. Thinking that they were safe, the outlaws had driven the cattle into a natural ampitheatre, formed by a circle of hills, and camped for the rest of the night. This was their undoing for Ralston and Andrew caught sight of their campfire and were able to creep up on them. Before the outlaws had a chance to counterattack seven were killed outright and the rest fled into the darkness.

None of Ralston's or Andrew's men were injured. They had taken the precaution of having several of their men watch the cattle and horses to prevent them stampeding during the fighting.

"Luck was with us tonight," Andrew said, "I feared we would lose men and cattle before we were finished. But there's scarce a man hurt and all the cattle are safe."

"Aye, it was the surprise that did it. They were fools to light a fire."

"They never thought we'd come after them in the dark. They thought they were safe 'til morning."

" 'Twas the surprise. They weren't ready for us this time. I'm going to look through the gear they left behind. We might find out who they are." Ralston said.

"I'll come and help you, the sooner we're out of here the better."

There seemed little of any value, "They had no provisions so they weren't expecting to go very far." Andrew said. "Their lair must be close by."

"Do you think the Urquarts know anything of them?"

"No, we have no quarrel with them."

"Then who?"

"God knows, as soon as a man has property, there's someone wanting to take it from him."

"Look, Andrew, Look in this sack!" and Ralston held open a small, rough sack which he had picked up from the ground. "Where do you think they got this?"

Andrew peered inside,

"Holy Virgin! Its all jewels! There's a fortune in there!"

"Well, its ours now. We'll share it equally."

"Aye, but not here, we'd better take it along and share it out when we get back." Andrew put his hand into the sack and brought out a handful of gold and then let it slip slowly back again.

"That'll be best. I'll put the sack across my saddle, we're ready to ride, aren't we?"

"The men can bring the cattle in the morning. I'll go and tell Robby to take over." And Andrew went to talk with the man who had been his right hand for years.

Ralston was back in his own home by daybreak and after tending to his horse, he wasted no time taking the sack to his bedchamber. Impatient to see the contents, he poured bracelets, necklets, earbobs, a dagger with a jewelled handle, golden gear of all kinds as well as gold and silver coins, on to the bed and stood looking at the treasure. He had never seen so much in one place. It was incredible but one thing seemed to Ralston to be more beautiful than anything else. It was a cross of gold inlaid with precious stones. Graceful and delicate, only about six inches high, it held Ralston spellbound.

He was different from most men of his age who had little time for works of art or things of beauty. Ralston loved beautiful things and got an almost sensuous pleasure from them. Tears would come to his eyes sometimes when he watched the golden dawn light up the heather and gradually lift the shadows from the hills. Sometimes he would stand and watch the sunset from the tall rocks close by. No one suspected this side of Ralston's nature. He went to great lengths to keep his feelings to himself. Only to Jean had he revealed something of his inner feelings and he wished she were with him to see these treasures.

Reluctantly, he laid the cross on the table by his bed and then put all the rest back into the sack tying the leather thong securely around the top. Then he picked up the cross and took it to the window to look at it more closely. Where had it come from? It must be from some holy place, but he had never seen or heard of such a cross before. Then he heard the horses coming towards the house. Thinking it might be the outlaws, Ralston slipped the cross into his sporran and ran down the stairs to put the sack in a secret place in the back of a closet.

It was none to soon, the horsemen were knocking at the gate by the time he had done. To Ralston's relief it was Andrew and two of his men.

"I didn't expect you so soon, but come on in."

"I thought we should share out before they could come back looking for it," Andrew said.

"You're right. Come up to my room, we won't be disturbed there."

Ralston went to get the sack from the closet as Andrew went up to his private chamber. Andrew and Ralston had spent so much time together that Andrew knew every corner of the house. His two men waited below with orders to look out for the outlaws.

"They'll be covering every inch of the ground looking for that sack," Ralston said, throwing it on the bed.

"They'll know we've got it and they'll be back, so the sooner we share out and lie low for a while, the better. Fifty-fifty and we each pay off our own men? What do you say?"

"Agreed, but why do you think they'll come here? Do you think they recognized me in the darkness?"

"They may not have, but we'd better be careful," Andrew said emptying the treasure on to the bed.

Both were silent for a moment as they looked at the wealth of gold, silver and jewels.

"God's Blood! What luck to come across that sack!"

"Aye, I picked it up only by chance. I thought it might be food, then when it was so heavy, I looked inside."

They started counting out the coins and putting them into two heaps. Then the necklets and other ornaments. Then Andrew looked puzzled and picking up the sack, he shook it out on to the bed.

"Looking for more?" Ralston joked. "Aren't you satisfied yet?"

"There was a cross. I saw it last night. Did it fall on the floor?" He bent down looking under the bed. Then he looked at Ralston accusingly,

"Where is it? Did you think I wouldn't miss it? I know it was there. I saw it. You were going to keep it for yourself, weren't you? You're nothing but a thief."

Ralston's face whitened with rage. Nobody had ever spoken to him like this and for Andrew, his friend to do it was incredible.

"You'd better take that back," he grated through his teeth, his hands clenching and unclenching in an effort to keep himself under control.

"I'm not taking anything back. You'd better give me that cross now or it'll be the worse for you."

Ralston no longer tried to control his anger. He had forgotton the cross until Andrew mentioned it. Flinging himself on Andrew he knocked him to the ground.

"Take that back or I'll kill you" Ralston shouted his hands pressing on Andrew's windpipe.

"Never." Andrew gasped and with desperate strength he pulled one arm free and jabbed his fist in Ralstons eye.

"God's Blood" Ralston screamed, releasing his hold on Andrew's throat. "You'll pay for this, take your gold and get out."

"I'm not going until I get that cross, you thief."

"You'll never get it now. Your filthy hands are not fit to touch it. Take your share and get out before I have my men throw you out."

Andrew sullenly gathered up his share into the sack.

"You'll not get away with this. I'll brand you as a thief before the world. I'll ruin you."

Ralston laughed.

"It's your word against mine. Why would anyone believe you and not me? You should think yourself lucky to be alive. I found that sack. I offered you a share. I brought my men to help you get your cattle back and how do you thank me? By calling me a thief. That's your way of thanking me? Never again will I call you friend."

When Andrew and his men were gone, Ralston's anger and indignation lessened, but the insult and mistrust had hurt him deeply. Like all Scotsmen he was very proud of his honor and good name. Such an insult could not easily be wiped out. It was even worse when it came from a friend.

All that day Ralston brooded over the wrong done to him by Andrew. Surely he would return and beg his forgiveness. But Andrew was just as angry, convinced that Ralston had intended to keep the cross for himself and not even tell him it was there. How much else had he helped himself to, Andrew wondered. If he would take one thing, he would take more.

Days passed and each brooded over their wrongs. Ralston did not even ride over to see Jean, though he was in the habit of seeing her several times a week. Then, ten days later, one of Andrew's men rode up with a message from Andrew. He wanted Ralston to meet him near the ruins of Redcastle on the Black Isle to see if they could resolve their differences. Ralston's first reaction was to refuse, then, reluctantly he agreed. "Tell you master I will meet him there." he said never dreaming of the horror that lay ahead.

It was a glowering day when Ralston, with but two of his men, rode to the Black Isle. He wondered why Andrew had chosen this place. True, it was isolated and no one would disturb them, then he shrugged, what did it matter where they met, Andrew must have come to his senses and wanted to put things right. Treachery did not enter Ralston's mind.

When Ralston arrived he found that Andrew was already there. He had six men with him. They had a fire burning and a small pot stood beside it. Still Ralston had no suspicions of foul play. They're probably going hunting later and that's why Andrew wanted to meet here.

Ralston dismounted and Andrew walked to meet him,
"Have you brought it?" he asked abruptly.
"Brought what?
"You know what I mean. The cross you stole, what else?"
Rage surged through Ralston and he shouted,
"Ye'll never get it. It's mine."
"That's your last word then? I'm warning you, you'll rue it."
"It's my only word." and turning on his heel Ralston made towards his horse intending to ride away.

"Seize him." Andrew shouted and, before Ralston could defend himself, four of Andrew's men leapt on him and pinned him to the ground. Leaving the horses, Ralston's men rushed to his aid but, before they could reach him, Andrew raised his pistol and fired two shots. Both men fell to the ground and lay still. Ralston fought like a demon, but he was unarmed and no match for the seven for them.

"Bring me the axe." Andrew shouted and put that pot back on the fire.

For the first time, Ralston realized that Andrew intended to kill him in cold blood. A chill of fear cooled his rage for a moment as he remembered the streak of madness that ran through this branch of the Stewart Clan. Too late he understood. Andrew was like a mad dog, he was completely crazy.

"Andrew, think what you're doing. You must be out of your mind. You can't get away with this."

"So you're ready to talk now, are you? Well its too late."

"And so you're going to kill me. How will you face your sister, my betrothed?"

"She'll want no more to do with ye, dead or alive. She will not marry a thief and I'm not killing you. Oh no, I've something better for you. I'm going to cut off your hands, that's the just punishment for thieves."

"You're insane! For God's sake Andrew! Stop this."

Andrew turned away, and shouted to his men,

"Bring him over to the stone." The two men dragged Ralston struggling and kicking to a flat boulder.

"Hold him down"

"Andrew, for the Love of God stop this madness." Ralston shrieked. But Andrew took no notice,

"Be still, you fool" he ordered as Ralston struggled to free himself. "Be still or you'll lose your arm along with your hand."

With growing horror Ralston saw the gleam in Andrew's eyes as he raised the axe. It was the sadistic pleasure of the torturer. He WAS mad, crazy!

"Kill me if you must, but leave my hands. For God's sake Andrew, leave my hands."

The axe fell and Ralston's unbelieving eyes saw his hand, his own, precious hand fall to the earth as the blood gushed out of his mutilated arm.

Andrew picked it up and threw if to one of his men.

"Keep it while I take the other." he shouted maliciously.

"No! No! Ralston shouted as they stretched out his other arm, "No!" struggling with energy born of desperation he tried to pull his arm away.

But the axe fell again and in agony Ralston rolled over, but they hadn't finished yet.

Grabbing the bleeding stumps the men poured some scalding pitch over them. Ralston screamed with agony as the violent pain tore through him. Then, his lungs exploding with one more terrible cry, he lost consciousness.

"That should finish the job." Andrew said then, hearing hoofbeats, he turned quickly and saw it was one of Ralston's men galloping away on Ralston's prized stallion. "Go after him and finish him" shouted Andrew. "God's Blood, why didn't you fools make sure they were dead. Where's my pistol? I'll make sure this one is done for." And going over to the man still lying on the ground, Andrew shot him through the head.

Hastily mounting their horses the men galloped off after the fugitive. But he had a good start and Ralston's horse was famous for its speed and surefootedness. This man, known as Old Rab, had been with

Ralston's family for many years and had practically brought up Ralston. Although he had been wounded, the shot had only grazed Rab's right side. But he was wily enough to play dead and wait until he could be of me help to his master. When he saw that Andrew had put down his pistols and he and his men were concentrating on their torture of Ralston, Old Rab saw his chance to get away. Old Rab intended to get help and come back to his master without delay, but Andrew and his men were hard on his heels and he knew they would not rest until they caught him. He was the only witness to the crime and the only one who could bring them to justice.

He rode furiously, urging on the willing horse. There was a close friend of Ralston's about a mile away and he knew he would give him shelter if he could reach there before Andrew and his men caught up with him. Luck was with him, for one of the violent storms that suddenly come up in that area darkened the sky and rain began to fall in torrents. While the lightning was revealing, the stormclouds hid Old Rab from view and made it possible to reach his refuge.

"I must speak to your master urgent." he gasped to the servant who came to see who was riding up. The man recognized him immediately and went to fetch his master.

"What's wrong, Rab? Come along in" and turning to the servant he said, "Take the horse to the stable and tend to him "Now Rab, tell me what's wrong. Here drink this" and the Laird of Dunmore handed Old Rab a glass of whiskey.

As Rab told his terrible tale, Dunmore could hardly contain his horror. "Was your master dead or alive when ye rode off?"

"I couldna tell, I had to move so fast. There was naught I could do to help him meself so I came to get help. They're after me. 'Twas only the storm coming up that let me get here without them seeing me."

"Aye, they'll want to stop ye from telling all. You're the only witness to this terrible thing. I'll go and search for your master. He may still be alive and laying out on the heather. Are you sure they didn't see you come here?"

"Aye, I'm sure. If they knew they'd be here by now. I'm afeared for my wife more than for meself."

"They'll watch your home for sure, but they won't harm her, its you they want. I'll take you to a place where they'll not find you and then I'll be on my way."

Without losing any time Dunmore led Rab to a secret hiding

place deep in one of the thick walls of the cellar. "You'll be safe here and I'll see to your wound when I return. Did any but Tam see you ride up?"

"No,"

"He'll hold his tongue. I'll give him warning." Dunmore rode hard through the storm to the place Old Rab had described. First he saw the body of one of Ralston's men. One quick look told him the man was dead and then riding a little further he saw, in a huddled heap near a large boulder, what was left of Ralston Munro.

At first he feared he was dead. Then when he dismounted and knelt beside him he saw Ralston's agonized eyes open and look at him without any recognition.

"It's me Dunmore, my friend. I've come to take you home. I'll help you mount my horse and we'll soon be there."

"No, Leave me here to die and swear ye'll never speak of this disgrace that's fallen on me. Go, leave me and forget you ever saw me here." and Ralston lay back on the heather exhausted.

"I will not leave you. You'll surely die here and from what Old Rab tells me, you need to live an take your revenge."

"Rab is alive? They didn't kill him?"

"No, now let me help you up."

"No, noone must see me like this. Leave me be, my friend. Its for the best."

In spite of all Dunmore's persuadings, Ralston refused to let him move him. Then at last he agreed to have Dunmore help him to the ruins of the castle, "It'll give you some shelter at least."

Half carrying him, Dunmore got Ralston into a place deep in the ruins which offered shelter form the weather.

"I'll be back with some bedding and other gear. And I'll try and get Doctor Benton to come to see to your wounds."

"No. Swear to me that you'll tell no one of my plight. I cannot have disgrace brought upon my name. If I live, I'll seek revenge, but until then, swear you will tell no one."

Seeing that Ralston's mind was set, Dunmore swore the oath. He knew Ralston would not survive without help and he must humor him or he would be dead in a few hours. The shock and loss of blood was enough to kill most men, but Ralston was so strong that Dunmore thought he could survive and get his revenge. And so the long years of Ralston's incredible sufferings began.

At first, he lay like an animal hidden in the dark, then gradually he began to move around in the ruins slowly regaining his strength. Dunmore came every day and fed him for Ralston could not bear any pressure on the stumps of his arms. Dunmore noticed that part of the forefinger and all the thumb was left on the right hand. When Andrew had brought the axe down, Ralston's struggles had prevented him from making a clean cut across the wrist as he had done with the left hand. Then the sound of Old Rab galloping away had made Andrew anxious to finish the job and get after Rab so he did not stop to make another cut with the axe. Even this did not comfort Ralston, but later he was to find that it made it possible for him to do some things for himself, when the stumps healed. The pitch stopped too much loss of blood and also infection, so although the sight of the black tar mixed with blood and bits of skin was impossible to look at without retching, healing began in time.

But Ralston still refused to let anyone know where he was.

"Its better that they think I am dead, than disgraced" he insisted.

Between them Rab and Dunmore kept Ralston alive through the worst, but Rab could only come in the dead of night as he was afraid of Andrew or his men catching him. Dunmore had many duties to attend to and occasionally had to spend time in Glasgow or London, so they worked out a system of providing Ralston with enough food and water for a week or more at a time.

When several weeks went by and Andrew had not found Old Rab or any sign of Ralston being still alive, he spread the tale that Ralston had stolen valuables from him and when he knew that Andrew had found out, Ralston was so ashamed that he left the country. Jean did not believe this at first, but when she went to Ralston's home to try to see him, the servants said he had left in a hurry and had not returned.

Ralston's family refused to believe that he would do anything wrong but Andrew was so convincing that they were forced to accept Andrew's explanation for his friend's absence. Especially when Andrew's men confirmed his story. "Why didn't you tell us before? Why did you wait so long?" Jean asked accusingly.

"I was hoping he would come back and then you need never have known about it. We could have settled everything between ourselves."

Brokenhearted, Jean and Ralston's father went through his belongings and, when they found the treasure, they thought it must be the valuables that belonged to Andrew. Andrew came hastily when they told him, hoping to find the cross. When he saw it wasn't there, he burst into a torrent of abuse.

Jean was shocked, she had never heard her brother speak in this way. It must be because he was so upset over all that had happened.

"How can you speak like that about Ralston? He is my betrothed and your friend."

"He is no longer my friend and I won't have my sister think of marrying a thief. In any case he's gone. That shows he's too ashamed to face you."

"I am sure that he will come back and then everything will be all right." Jean was crying now and John Munro put his arm around her and said,

"Don't let Andrew upset you like this. I am sure that we will find out the truth sooner or later. If this is not your gear, Andrew, you'd better leave this house. I don't want to hear from you until you are able to speak kindly of my son."

"You'd side with a thief would you?"

"Until we hear the whole story from Ralston, we will not believe ill of him."

Andrew flung himself out of the house muttering under his breath, leaving Jean and John Munro to gather up the treasure.

"We'd better keep this in a safe place until Ralston comes back. But I may have to use some of the money to pay his servants. They should be taken care of. He would want that done."

"Yes, especially Old Rab and the widow of Malcolm, he had been with Ralston about five years, hadn't he?"

"Yes, for the time being I had forgotten about him. His family should be provided for."

When the years went by and Ralston still did not return, people began to believe that Andrew was speaking the truth. But Jean remained faithful, even though it seemed that everything was against Ralston. She did not marry anyone else. In fact, she scarcely went to any functions where there were people of her own age. Dunmore and Old Rab did their best to persuade Ralston to come home, but it was useless.

"I'm biding my time, I'm waiting until the time is ripe and then I'll force him to admit the truth. I know it will come about and, I will stay alive until that happens and then I can die in peace." Ralston's voice was so weak it was like the moaning of the wind in winter. He had grown so thin that he seemed no more than skin covered bones. It broke Dunmore's heart to look at him. Ralston saw the sorrow on his friend's face and said,

"Don't grieve for me, dear friend, I am grieving for you who have to care for me and for Rab here who has to keep hidden and dare not share his wife's bed."

"You need good food, not this dried stuff I have to bring. You haven't slept in a clean bed for years. I cannot bear to see you so. For a common man it would not be so hard, but for you, so gently bred—" Dunmore shook his head.

"My time will come. I'll get my revenge. "Til then I'll stay here."

"Won't you wear the new plaid I brought? That old thing is filthy and in rags."

"I must take my revenge in the clothes I had that day. The dried blood is to remind Andrew of what he did."

His mind is turned. Dunmore thought sadly, but he tried again to get Ralston to come back with him,

"We can bring Old Rab to bear witness to what happened on that day. That should be proof."

"I want my revenge on Andrew. Look at these arms, these mangled limbs! Don't I deserve revenge? In any case, Rab would only be one against Andrew and seven of his men. Do you think Rab would be believed? You know they would believe Andrew before a serving man. Then they would kill him. That's what they're waiting for. Rab's the only witness I have, but he can't stand alone."

Dunmore had to admit that Ralston was right, but he hated to have Ralston rot away in the filth and darkness of the ruins. How much longer could he stand it? As far as Dunmore could tell there was no way Ralston could take revenge on Andrew. He was helpless. Dunmore also hated to face John Munro and keep the secret of his son's whereabouts from him. Still more he hated to met Jean's sad, blue eyes and hear her speak of the days when she rode across the heather to meet Ralston. What would be the end of it all? The time would come when neither he nor Rab could continue to provide for Ralston. Then what would happen to him? Also, as Ralston had said, Old Rab and his wife dared only to meet in lonely places from time to time. They were growing too old for all this.

After thinking it over for some weeks, Dunmore took Old Rab into his confidence,

"I've made up my mind to tell Jean the whole story. She's the only one that could make your master return home. Maybe he'll come to his senses when he sees she's been faithful and lonely all these years."

"But the shock of it all might kill her. She's only a lassie after all. And the sight of him! That's enough to send her running in fright.

"I know all that, Rab, but Jean's a strong girl and I'll tell her his condition before she sees him so it won't be such a shock. If I know her, she'll be overjoyed to know he's alive and faithful no matter what state he's in. What else can we do? He can't go on like this forever, neither can you. You're entitled to your own hearth and home and, until this is settled, you're as much an exile as he is."

"Well, its true, I do pine for my hearth and home. My bones ache at night on the damp heather and not being able to see my own kin is hard, very hard. If ye think its the way to go, I can't go against ye."

So Dunmore invited Jean over to his home on a day when his good wife was away visiting relatives. He did not want to run the risk of his wife learning of Ralston's trouble after giving his oath to Ralston never to betray him. He knew his wife would take matters in her own hands and, as she was a determined and heavy handed lady, she would probably go forth and try and settle things to her own fancy and the detriment of all concerned.

Jean was surprised to be invited, but the families had known each other for many years, so she rode over wondering what Dunmore could want.

Somehow she looked more fragile than Dunmore had expected and he almost lost his determination to tell her. Then the picture of Ralston in his tattered plaid wasting his life and suffering such misery and pain restored his courage and he began his story.

He had taken the precaution of having a decanter of whiskey and some glasses on a tray close by thinking they might both need it. But, although Jean's face whitened and tears rolled down her cheeks, she bravely listened through to the end.

"Dear God!" she cried "How could such a terrible thing happen? How could my own brother be guilty of such horror? Such cruelty! And Ralston alone in degradation and suffering all these years! Its more than anyone can bear. But I thank God he is alive and I will care for him and love him and make up for all these lost years." Her face was joyous she did not even consider anything but going directly to Ralston and bringing him home with her.

"Let us go now. We mustn't leave him there another hour." she cried.

"We must be very careful, my dear, Ralston is very proud and he is changed from what he was. Now all that he can think about is revenge. I don't want him to break your heart by refusing to go with you. We must plan how best to approach him."

"Ralston would never change so completely. He would never turn against me. Let us go."

"We must wait for night. We cannot risk Andrew or any of his men following us."

"Andrew is sure he is dead. And he doesn't suspect that you know anything, does he?"

"Not as far as I know, but he is very suspicious of everyone . . . Tell me my dear, do you think he has become somewhat strange of late?"

"He has become very suspicious and he is ready to fight or quarrel with anyone. Now I can understand why. With such a thing on his mind, its a wonder he hasn't become even worse. What can these valuables be that he thinks Ralston stole from him? He had no valuables. My mother has her jewels but they are to come to me and, all else is to be shared when my parents die. Andrew has nothing of his own apart from his cattle."

"Ralston can tell you the story better than I can. But this is roughly what happened," and Dunmore told Jean as much as he knew.

"But if Ralston found the treasure, it was all his. He didn't have to share it. And the cross? What happened to it?"

"I don't know. Well, my dear, is your mind made up to go now or, shall we talk over a plan?"

"I can't wait another hour. Let's go now. We can leave a message to say we have gone riding and then they won't miss us."

"You're sure you can stand it? His mutilated arms, his filthy appearance. His long hair and beard. He is not the young, handsome man you knew."

"Don't worry, and don't take any notice of my tears or anything else. Its just so hard to believe that I hardly know what I am doing. But I am so happy at the thought of seeing him again. But, tell me" her voice changed to fear, "Will he blame me for what my brother did? Does he hate our whole family? How does he speak of me?"

"He does not hate you. Its Andrew he hates." Dunmore didn't want to admit that Ralston had not spoken of Jean.

Dunmore went to order the horses to be brought around but, just as Jean was mounting, a horseman was seen galloping to the house.

"Get inside, Jean while I see who it is. He's in a great hurry. Something must be wrong."

Reluctantly Jean went back inside, but before she could close the door, Dunmore called to her and she saw the horseman was one of her father's men.

"What is it, Jamie? Is anything wrong?"

"It's Master Andrew. The Laird and your mother need you to home. Ye'd best come right away."

"What's happened to Andrew?" Jean asked fearful of more bad news.

"He was in a fight coming back from Glasgow and he was shot in the head. They brought him back dead, Miss Jeanie."

"Dead! Andrew's dead?" suddenly Jean felt faint, so much had happened in the last hour that she was dazed.

"Come, sit here and rest a few minutes and you too, Jamie, John will see to the horses while you go round to the kitchen for a drappie. Miss Jean needs a few moments before she rides back with you."

"I'll be all right, it was just such a shock after what you had just told me about Ralston. I can't believe that Andrew is dead. This changes everything, doesn't it?"

"Yes, its unbelievable I know, but it makes everything easier. You must go home with Jamie and I will go to Ralston this evening and tell him about Andrew. I hope he will come back with me and then Old Rab can go home at last."

"What about Andrew's men? Do you think they will cause trouble?"

"They'll run like rabbits, they will be afraid of what Old Rab and Ralston will do to them when they know they are alive and Andrew is dead. Without Andrew they have no protection and they know it."

"Poor Andrew, he is my brother. Before all this trouble we had many happy days together with Ralston. I never thought it would come to this. I'd better go to my mother, she will never believe any ill of Andrew. He was her favorite. It will break her heart."

"Do you feel able to ride now?"

"Yes, I'm all right now. Tell Ralston of my love for him won't you? And you will come and tell me when I can see him?"

"Yes I will come over tomorrow in any case. I don't know what Ralston will want to do. He is so changed."

"Try and make him come home. Tell him I am waiting to marry him."

"I will do that my dear. Now you'd better be going and I will carry your messages tonight."

At first Ralston could not take in what Dunmore was telling him. "You really mean that Andrew is dead? Killed by a pistol wound? Are you sure? You don't think its a ruse to smoke us out?"

"No, I don't think so. Jamie had seen him and he said he was dead from a pistol shot through the head.

"God be praised. The earth is free from a mad tyrant at last. But I wish he had died a lingering death. I wanted to make him suffer as he made me suffer."

"Remember the bible, Ralston, Vengeance is mine, saith the Lord. Let us look to the future. I saw Jean today and I told her you were still alive and that I knew where you are and she told me to tell you that she is still waiting to marry you. She loves you still, no matter what has happened to you."

Dunmore was totally unprepared for Ralston's reaction. He had expected him to refuse to come back, to be angry that he had broken his oath and told Jean he was alive, anything, but what happened. To his sorrow Ralston collapsed on the ground and burst into violent sobs which wracked his fragile body and tore into Dunmore's own composure. It was if all the sufferings of the past ten years were taking their toll.

Dunmore did not try to stop Ralston's tears, even though he feared the emotion might be too much for him. He needs to get it out of his system. He's held it in all these years, he thought. In a few minutes Ralston lay still.

"Forgive me, old friend. It won't happen again" Ralston said.

"There's nothing to forgive. You have suffered too much. Its good to let it out. It cleanses the mind and body. Rest there, while I tell you what I propose you do. Will you hear me out?"

"I'll hear you. You have been my friend and borne with me all these years. Without you and Old Rab I would have died like a dog with none to mourn me."

"You would have done the same for me, I know that. The best way to repay me is to let me see you and Jean together and Rab back with his wife. I want you to come back with me tonight to my place and have a bath and then get a good night's sleep in a comfortable bed. Then tomorrow have a haircut so, when Jean comes to see you, she isn't frightened at the sight of you. With Andrew dead, there's no more need to stay here. You owe it to Jean, to your family and to me as well as yourself, to get back and start being a useful Scotsman again. What do you say?"

"Ralston raised his face still stained with tears and said,

"You would not deceive me on such a thing would you? Jean truly said she loves me still? She didn't believe that I stole from Andrew?"

"I would not deceive you about a thing like this, Jean has been true to you all these years. If the news of Andrew's death had not come as we were starting out, she would have come with me to try and get you to come back. She is waiting for you."

"Its so strange, I can hardly believe that all this is happening. And what is strangest of all, I no longer want my revenge. Andrew took all my hatred with him."

"Then you'll come with me?"

"Gladly, but there is one thing I must do." And Ralston fumbled in his ragged sporran and brought out something that flashed and glittered in the light of the lantern. It was the cross.

"What is it?"

"It's the cause of all the trouble." Ralston showed it to Dunmore, then he flung it back into the ruins as far as he could. "I never want to see it again. It is accursed. Now I am ready, I have nothing to take from this place as you well know."

Dunmore had to lift Ralston on to the saddle in front of him. He was much weaker than Dunmore had realized. I hope he lives through all this. It would be a terrible thing if we got him back only to die on our hands, he thought.

But Dunmore need not have worried. The following morning Ralston bathed, rested and dressed in decent clothing once more, looked very much alive. He was wearing a shirt with cuffs that came down over his wrists hiding the stumps of his arms. He was able to hold a fork with the finger and thumb of his right hand and feed himself. He looked quite different. "I sent a messenger to bring Jean over because I know how anxious she is to see you. No one except Old Rab knows you're here as yet."

"I feel as nervous as a schoolboy at seeing her again."

"You won't be nervous when you see her. Look, here they come."

In a moment Jean was through the door and catching sight of

Ralston she flung herself into his arms. He had no chance to say anything or think even. His arms went around her naturally as her head sank on his shoulder and her tears fell on his chest. Dunmore took one look and then slipped out with a full and thankful heart.

Ralston and Jean were married shortly after Andrew's funeral and they went to live in Ralston's house. Old Rab returned to his home and came back to do light work for Ralston as long as he lived.
The couple never went back to The Black Isle and as far as is known, the jewelled cross is still lying in the ruins, forgotton.

Treasure Hunting Information

Before digging for treasure in any country it is well to find out whether the property is privately owned or part of public lands. If you want to dig or search on private property, be sure to ask permission of the owner or landlord. Agree to split with him if you find anything and be sure to get any arrangement in writing. If land is publicly owned, the law varies from country to country and state to state.

In Scotland all Treasure Trove belongs to the Crown if the owner is unknown. The Queen may grant the Treasure Trove to another if she so wishes.

TREASURE TROVE is any gold or silver in coin, plate or bullion found concealed in a house, or in the earth or any other private place, the owner being unknown; (Chitty, Law of the Prerogatives of the Crown 152.)

Ownership is decided by a Coroner's Court. The duty of the Coroner with regard to treasure trove is to go where the treasure is found and to issue a warrant for summoning a jury to appear before him in a certain place in the same manner as he issues him warrant to summon a jury to hold an inquest on a dead body.

Treasure Trove may be granted by the Crown in the form of a franchise, but as it belongs to the Crown by virtue of prerogative and therefore does not exist as franchise until specialy created, it must be expressly named.

If the finder of a treasure trove reports the find promptly and hands over the treasure to the proper authorities, Her Majesty, in the right of the Duchy of Lancaster, or the Duke of Cornwall in the right of the Duchy of Cornwall, will pay to the finder the full market value if it is retained by the Crown. If it is not retained, the finder will receive all objects back with full liberty to do what he likes with them, or if he wishes it, the British Museum will sell them for him at the best price obtainable. If the coroner decides that more than one person was concerned in the finding, the reward may be divided, but the reward is made to the actual finder or finders and not to the owner of the land.

The best way to report a find is through the police who will inform the coroner on request.

WRECKS. Where any person finds or takes possession of any wreck within the United Kingdom, or, having found it outside the United Kingdom, brings it within the United Kingdom, then, if he is the owner, he must give notice of it, or, if he is not the owner, he must deliver the same, to the receiver of wrecks for the district appointed by the Secretary of State for the Environment, in the prescribed manner.

EQUIPMENT. A treasure hunters needs vary with the type of treasure he is hunting and the type of countryside where it is hidden. But here are a few general hints for Scottish areas. Scotland is chilly and damp except for July and August as a rule, so wear warm clothing and have something waterproof. The terrain is rugged so you will need good strong boots. Of course, there is a good supply of Scotch Whiskey everywhere which the locals use for warmth.

DETECTORS. Detectors can be hired in Scotland, but as many of the treasure spots are remote, it is better to take your own. We have had no luck with the dowsing instruments some treasure hunters spend money on, we have done better with a metal detector of the type which sends out a balanced electromagnetic field. Whites, Garrett's, Master hunter, Compass are all good and have a variety of types at various prices.

MAPS AND COMPASSES. The official maps of Scotland easily available in shops and newsstands in the British Isles are excellent. They give all the help a map can give.

You will need a good compass to get your bearings. Also a surveyor's tape to measure distances.

TRANSPORTATION. The railroad service is fairly good but infrequent in parts of Scotland. There are buses but they do not run every day to the treasure areas, so it is better to rent a car or station wagon and drive yourself. You can arrange this when you buy your airline ticket.

ACCOMMODATIONS. Scotland, like England has excellent little places where simple bed and breakfast is supplied at a very reasonable rate. A list of such places can be obtained from British Travel Agencies.

DO NOT GO TREASURE HUNTING ALONE. If you had an accident in a remote area, no one might find you for days. Take a friend.

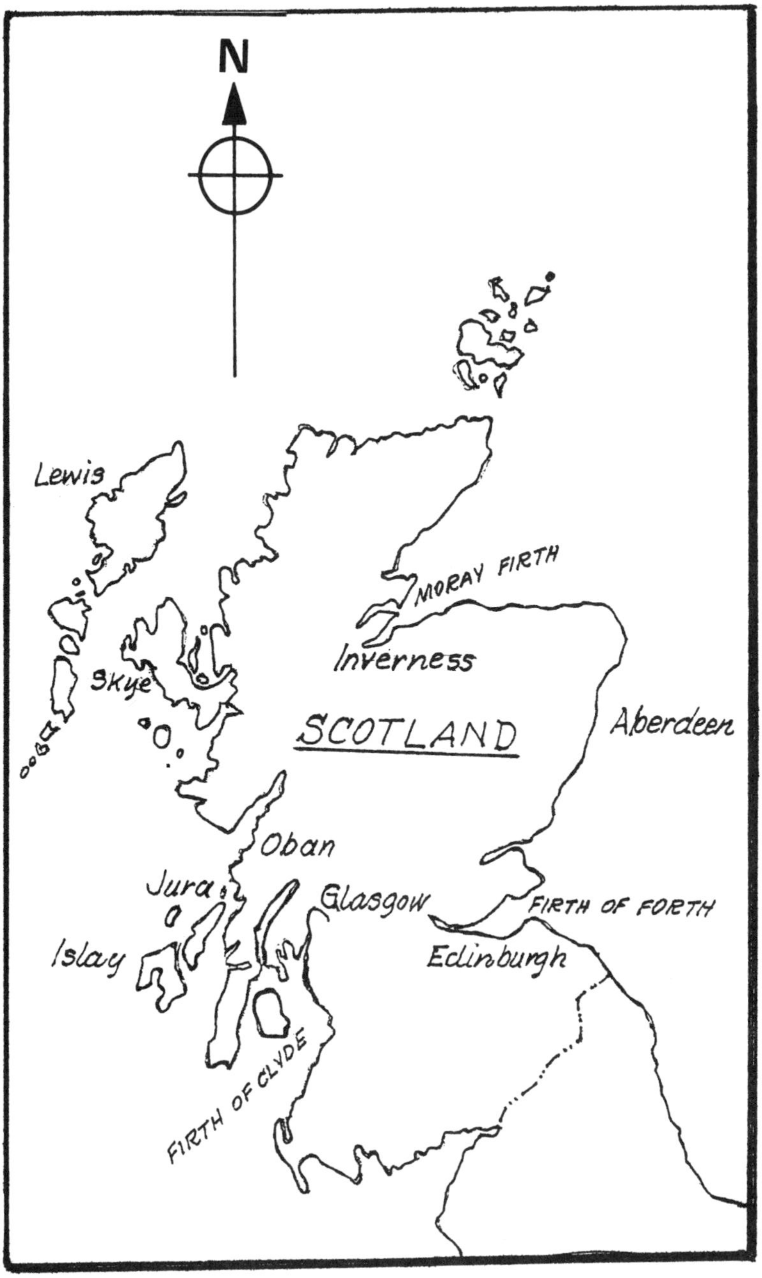
N
Lewis
MORAY FIRTH
Inverness
Skye
SCOTLAND
Aberdeen
Oban
Jura
Glasgow
FIRTH OF FORTH
Islay
Edinburgh
FIRTH OF CLYDE

Jack Forbes is a student of history and enjoys the old tales of Scotland. He always spend his vacation in the Scottish Highlands or the Hebrides. He contributes articles on Scotland to various magazines.

P.B. Innis is the author of 14 books. GOLD IN THE BLUE RIDGE which was written with Walter Innis, is a favorite of treasure hunters everywhere. The Innis's are experienced treasure hunters. Their adventures have been the subject of many national TV programs and documentaries. P.B.Innis' articles on treasure have appeared in Argosy magazine, Das Tier and Treasure magazine.

The maps in this book were drawn by Walter Innis whose maps appear in the works of Samuel Elliott Morrison.